110 CARD GAMES
FOR EXPERT PLAYERS

110 CARD GAMES
FOR EXPERT PLAYERS

History, rules and winning strategies for bridge, whist, hearts, canasta and many other games, with 200 photographs and diagrams

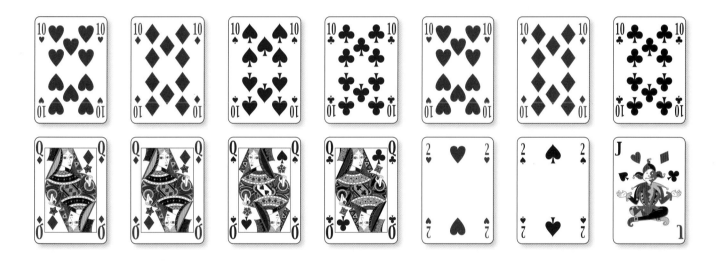

Jeremy Harwood

southwater

This edition is published by Southwater
an imprint of Anness Publishing Ltd
108 Great Russell Street
London WC1B 3NA
info@anness.com

www.southwaterbooks.com
www.annesspublishing.com

Anness Publishing has a new picture agency outlet
for images for publishing, promotions or advertising.
Please visit our website www.practicalpictures.com
for more information.

A CIP catalogue record for this book
is available from the British Library.

Designed and produced for Anness Publishing by
THE BRIDGEWATER BOOK COMPANY LIMITED

Publisher: Joanna Lorenz
Project Editors: Rosie Gordon and Felicity Forster
Project Manager: Polita Caaveiro
Editor: Nick Fawcett
Art Director: Lisa McCormick
Illustrations: Virginia Zeal
Designers: Stuart Perry and Sylvia Tate
Production Controller: Pirong Wang

Previously published as part of a larger volume,
How to Play the 200 Best-Ever Card Games

CONTENTS

INTRODUCTION

Dedicated card players are always on the lookout for games they have not played before. The card games in this book require more skill than the average, and so will appeal to the more sophisticated player rather than the complete beginner. This is not to say that a novice should never experiment – only that it is a good idea to master the principles of simpler trick-taking games, such as Whist, before trying to tackle a more complicated bidding game such as Contract Bridge.

Excellent Contract Bridge players have almost always started off with Whist, its 17th-century antecedent. Indeed, many experts believe that, while any good Whist player can become a good Bridge player once the elements of bidding have been mastered, many who pass as good Bridge players could be quite out of their depth at Whist. In fact, the British card authority David Parlett is of the opinion that 'nobody should learn Bridge without prior experience of Whist', going as far as to say that 'many Bridge players would improve their game by going on a crash diet of Whist only'.

QUICK-TRICK GAMES

Quick-trick games can also be very challenging. As in Bridge, many of these games include an element of bidding, but the element that makes them particularly demanding is that, as opposed to many other card games, not all the cards are dealt. Naturally, this makes it harder for players to deduce what cards their opponents may be holding.

Above: Well-dressed players taking part in a Whist drive, c.1906. The players change tables every few deals and face several different pairs of opponents.

Euchre, for which the modern Joker was invented, is the most sophisticated of these games, although Nap, or Napoleon, a simplified version, is probably more popular, being played throughout northern Europe under different guises. The author Jerome K. Jerome mentioned the game in his comic masterpiece *Three Men in a Boat*, when he described his three leading characters – J, the book's narrator, George and Harris – settling down to indulge in a game of 'Penny Nap after supper'. The game was probably named after the French emperor Napoleon III, who is thought to have played a version of it.

HEARTS AND ITS RELATIVES

Games in the Hearts family stand the usual scoring conventions of card games on their head. The aim in these games is to *avoid* winning tricks, and so amass points. This makes Twos and Threes as valuable as Aces and Kings often are in other card games, while holding middle-ranking cards, such as Sevens and Eights, can mean positive danger, if not complete disaster.

Playing games like Hearts well means cultivating a special kind of card sense. Often, it is best to aim not to take any tricks at all, especially in games where holding or winning certain cards means incurring a penalty. Two variants (not included in this book) illustrate this point well. In Black Maria, the player ending up with the

Above: A fashionable group play a game of Bridge, 1912.

Above: An international Bridge tournament in New York in 2005. Played socially by many, Bridge is also a seriously competitive game, with championship matches held across the world.

Queen of Spades scores an extra 13 points, and each Heart counts for a single point, although a player with the Jack of Diamonds deducts 12 points from his score. In Pink Lady, the other variant, ending up with the Queen of Hearts means a 13-point penalty.

In Jacks and its close relative Polignac, the Jacks, as might be expected, are the high-scoring danger cards.

ACES, TENS AND OTHER CARDS

Some card games give specific cards particular values. In games such as Skat, Germany's most popular card game, Aces count for 11 points, Tens 10, Kings four, Queens three and Jacks two. The aim is to win at least 61 card points in tricks (the number of tricks taken is in itself immaterial). So-called King-Queen games are governed by the same principles, and, in them, declaring the 'marriage' of a King and Queen of the same suit in the same hand wins bonus points. This makes games like Sixty-Six exciting because it introduces an element of unpredictability into the game. Declaring a 'marriage' can transform the scoring situation, turning a losing player into a winning one.

Games like Bezique, Marjolet and Pinochle use the same principles, with an extra 'marriage' being allowed between a specified Queen and a Jack of a different suit. They differ in the fact that players win most of their points by collecting and melding certain sequences and combinations of cards. In Jack-Nine games, the Jack is promoted to become the highest trump, followed by the Nine. The three classic examples of this type of game are Belote, Klaverjas and Schieber Jass, the national card games of France, the Netherlands and Switzerland, respectively.

POKER AND ITS ORIGINS

Of all these more advanced games, Poker stands alone. This is a five-card vying game in which players bet money or gambling chips into a communal pot during the course of a hand; the player who has the best hand at the end of the betting wins the pot, in a 'showdown'. It is also possible for the pot to be won by a hand that is not the best, by bluffing the other players out of play.

It is believed that Poker emerged early in the 19th century, probably in New Orleans, on board the great Mississippi paddle steamers. It seems likely that its immediate ancestor was a French game called Poque, which itself was a version of the German game Poch. According to American card authority Louis Coffin, 'the French name was pronounced 'poke' and Southerners corrupted the pronunciation to Pokuh or Poker'. Brag, a vying game based on three-card hands, is also thought to have been an influence.

By Victorian times, Draw and Stud Poker had emerged. Then came further variants in which the notion of one or more communal cards was introduced. By that time, Poker had become what American card historian Allen Dowling aptly termed 'the great American pastime'. It is now a favourite throughout the card-playing world.

Right: Classic image of a joker or court jester, wearing a cap and bells, carrying a ninny stick, or jester's wand, from a 15th-century manuscript.

7

1 | BRIDGE AND WHIST GAMES

BRIDGE AND WHIST BELONG TO TRICK-TAKING CARD GAMES, IN WHICH THE OBJECTIVE IS TO WIN A SPECIFIED NUMBER OF TRICKS; AS MANY TRICKS AS POSSIBLE; OR OCCASIONALLY A SPECIFIED ONE, SUCH AS THE LAST TRICK OF A HAND. IN SOME GAMES, THE AIM IS TO LOSE RATHER THAN WIN TRICKS, WHILE IN POINT-TRICK GAMES, THE TOTAL POINT VALUE OF THE CARDS TAKEN DETERMINES THE RESULT, RATHER THAN THE NUMBER OF TRICKS.

As far as most trick-taking games are concerned, the rules clearly state what can be led and when. The most common requirement is the need to follow suit. In certain games, players are required to ruff – that is, to play a trump – if they are unable to follow suit and hold a trump card or cards in their hands.

In trick play, each player is normally dealt the same number of cards and plays a card in turn face up to the table. The player with the best card, usually the highest-ranking card of the suit that has been led or the highest trump, wins all the others. These constitute a trick which the winner places face down in a winnings pile; he then plays the first card of the next trick. Who leads initially is normally decided by cutting the cards. The other players play in order according to their positions around the card table, typically clockwise in games from English-speaking countries. In positive trick-taking games, players aim to take as many tricks as possible. Exact prediction trick-taking games, such as Bridge, involve a contract, in which players aim to win a set number of tricks. There are two scoring systems. In what are termed plain-trick games, it is only the number of tricks taken by each player that matters. The points on the cards making up the tricks are irrelevant. In point-trick games, however, players are rewarded or penalized for capturing certain cards, each of which has a pre-assigned value.

Above: Harold Vanderbilt (1884–1970), American multi-millionaire, revised the rules of bridge in 1925, thus turning auction bridge into contract bridge.

CONTRACT BRIDGE

Love it or loathe it, Bridge has long been one of the most popular card games in the world: its origins date back to the 1880s. Auction Bridge made its debut in 1904 and Contract Bridge in 1925. The latter soon became the dominant form of the game, thanks largely to two Americans – Harold Vanderbilt, who codified its rules, and master player Ely Culbertson, the great popularizer of the game.

OBJECT

To make, in tandem with one's partner, a specified number (contract) of tricks – or more – scoring enough points over a sequence of deals to make game and then win a rubber without giving away a greater number of points in doing so. A rubber is card parlance for a match. It usually consists of three games and is won, or taken, by the first partnership to win two of them.

SPECIAL FEATURES

Establishing Partners

Partners are determined by social agreement, or by a cut, in which the cards are fanned out face down on the table. Each player in turn draws a card. The two players with the highest-scoring cards become the lead partnership; the player with the higher card becomes the dealer. The convention is to sit around the table according to the points of the compass – North and South form one partnership and East and West the other.

Dummy

After the first card of a hand has been led, the cards of the declarer's partner are laid face up on the table and he takes no active part in that particular hand. The declarer is the highest bidder at the auction (see page 135).

Ruffing

In Bridge, playing a trump is termed ruffing. Usually the declarer and the dummy (see above) control the majority of trumps between them since they chose the suit to be played. Thus, one of the declarer's aims is to draw off the opposing partnership's trumps, leaving them with none. The declarer normally has enough trumps left to make sure that the defending partnership is not given the opportunity to win tricks with what are termed long

You will need: 52-card deck; no Jokers; scorecards

Card ranking: Standard, Aces high

Players: Four, playing in partnerships of two

Ideal for: 14+

Above: Ely Culbertson (1891–1955) built on the efforts of the founders of Contract Bridge by developing the game's first comprehensive bidding system. The vast publicity campaign he orchestrated for Bridge was instrumental in establishing its popularity.

cards, as these will simply be trumped. Long cards are the cards remaining in a suit after all the cards of the other players have been exhausted.

SCORING

Both partnerships keep running scorecards, which are divided into two columns headed 'WE' and 'THEY' with a horizontal line partway down each sheet. Points can be scored 'above the line' and 'below the line'.

If a partnership wins a contracted number of tricks or more, it is deemed to have fulfilled its contract and a score is awarded accordingly. If not, the contract is said to be defeated and points are awarded to the defending partnership. Each partnership aims to win the most points in the best of the three games that make up a rubber.

Points per Trick

Trick points (only given for each trick over 'the book', which consists of the first six tricks) are entered below the line. Only the declaring partnership can score them and then only if it has fulfilled the contract for the deal. If trumps are Clubs or Diamonds, the partnership scores 20 per trick, and 30 per trick if trumps are Hearts or Spades. If there are No Trumps, it scores 40 for the first trick after the book and 30 for each subsequent one. Clubs and Diamonds are termed minor suits, while Hearts and Spades are the major suits.

Doubles and Redoubles

If the contract is doubled, scores are doubled in turn. If it is redoubled, points are multiplied by four. If the declaring partnership succeeds in winning a doubled contract, it wins an extra 50 points above the line. This is sometimes known as '50 for the insult'. The bonus above the line for a redoubled contract is 100 points.

SCORES AT CONTRACT BRIDGE

Contract made: the declarer scores below the line for each trick bid and won

Suit bid and won	Points	Doubled	Redoubled
Minor suit (♦ ♣)	20	40	80
Major suit (♠ ♥)	30	60	120
No Trump (NT) for 1st trick	40	80	160
NT for subsequent tricks	30	60	120

Declarers may also score above the line

(TV= trick value, V=Vulnerable)

	Points	Doubled	Redoubled
For each overtrick	TV	100	200
For each overtrick (V)	TV	200	400
For making a doubled/ redoubled contract	50	100	
For making a small slam	500/750 (V)		
For making a grand slam	1000/1500 (V)		

Contract defeated: the defenders score above the line

Undertricks	Points	Doubled	Redoubled
First	50	100	200 (if not vulnerable)
or	100	200	400 (if vulnerable)
Second/Third	50	200	400 (If not vulnerable)
or	100	300	600 (if vulnerable)
plus for each subsequent trick	0	100	200 (if not vulnerable)

Honours: scored above the line

Any four of A, K, Q, J, 10 of trumps	100
All five of A, K, Q, J, 10 of trumps	150
All four Aces at No Trumps	150

Rubber scores at the end of play

Winning the rubber, opponents winning one game	500
Winning the rubber, opponents winning no games	700
Winning the only game in an unfinished rubber	300
For the only part-score in an unfinished game	100

Bonus and Penalty Points

Bonuses for tricks made in excess of a contract, or points awarded to a defending partnership if the contract is defeated, are also recorded above the line. These are termed overtricks and undertricks. Overtricks are scored the same as bid tricks. If, however, a declaring partnership wins fewer tricks than it bid, neither side scores anything below the line, but the defending partnership scores above the line for the number of tricks by which the declaring partnership falls short of its target. The value of such scores varies, depending on whether a partnership is what is termed 'vulnerable'. If it is, the scores are increased. A partnership is deemed vulnerable once it has won a game towards a best-of-three rubber. Once the two partnerships have each won a game, they are both vulnerable.

Slams

A contract to make all 13 possible tricks is termed a Grand Slam, while a contract to make 12 is a Small Slam. If a declaring partnership is vulnerable, it wins a bonus of 750 points above the line for making a Small Slam and 1,500 for a Grand Slam. If it is not vulnerable, it wins 500 points or 1,000 points.

Honours

Bonus points are awarded to players holding honours in their hands before any cards are played, although these are not actually scored until the end of the hand. Honours are the top five trumps: Ace, King, Queen, Jack and Ten. If a player holds all of these, he scores a bonus of 150 points above the line for the partnership. Four honours in one hand score 100. If there are No Trumps, but a player holds four Aces, the partnership scores 150 points for honours.

Points when Vulnerable

A partnership that has won a game is deemed vulnerable, meaning that any penalty points incurred against it are significantly increased (see scoring table, left). Both partnerships can be vulnerable at the same time.

Game and Rubber

A rubber typically consists of three games, so is won by the first side to win two. If a partnership wins two games without reply, it scores 700 bonus points for the rubber, this being reduced to 500 points if the opposing partnership has won a game. Victory in the rubber, however, goes to the partnership with the highest total after trick and premium points have been added together.

HAND A

HAND B

HAND C

Above and left: In adding up the value of hands, Aces are worth four points, Kings three, Queens two and Jacks one. An extra point is added in Hand A for the doubleton (just two cards in a suit), two points for Hand B for the singleton (just one card), and three points for Hand C for the void (where one suit is absent).

THE DEAL

Each player is dealt 13 cards, the dealer distributing the cards clockwise, one at a time. After each hand, the deal passes to the player to the left of the previous dealer.

A hand needs to contain at least 12 points to be worth an opening bid, i.e. to be considered a winning hand. An Ace is worth four points, a King three, a Queen two and a Jack one. Some players allow an extra point for a five-card major suit, or for a 'doubleton' (two cards in a particular suit), adding two points for a 'singleton' (just one card in a suit) and three for a 'void' (where one suit is absent).

THE AUCTION AND CONTRACT

After the deal, the starting point is an auction, often termed bidding, which ends with the establishment of a contract. By this, the winning partnership commits itself to taking a minimum number of tricks, either with a specific suit as trumps or with No Trumps. The auction is started by the dealer when all the players have evaluated the cards in their hands, other players calling in clockwise order.

There are four types of call – bid, double, redouble and pass. A bid indicates the aim of making six tricks, the book, with one's partner, plus a stated number of extra ones, from one to seven, 'the levels'. A bid of 3♦ would mean that the bidder anticipates the partnership can take nine tricks in all (the book plus three), with Diamonds – the denomination – as the trump suit. An alternative would be 3NT (No Trumps), in which case the target is still nine tricks, but the hand is played without a trump suit.

A player can double the last bid by an opponent and redouble if the opponent's last bid was a double. If a doubled bid becomes the contract, the score for making it, plus any overtricks, is doubled, but penalty points are doubled likewise if the contract is not made. A pass means no bid. The auction is over if three passes in succession follow a bid, double or redouble, or if all four players pass in the first round of bidding. In the latter case, all the cards are thrown in and the player to the dealer's left shuffles and deals again.

When first bidding, the key aim is to find the strengths and weaknesses of other players' hands as well as trying to making a contract. All kinds of bidding systems have been devised to this end. Players must state which system they are using at the start of a rubber before play begins.

There are 35 possible bids in all. Each bid has to be higher than the previous one. The level – that is, the number of tricks the bidding partnership undertakes to win – can obviously be increased, in which case any denomination can be specified, or the denomination can be changed to a higher one, with the level remaining the same. Denominations are ranked, from lowest to highest, as Clubs, Diamonds, Hearts, Spades and No Trumps (NT). The lowest possible bid is 1♣, while 7NT is the highest.

PLAY

Once the auction is over and the contract established, the player in the contracting partnership who first bid No Trumps or a trump suit becomes the declarer, playing his partner's hand (the dummy) as well as his own. The partner lays his cards down face up on the table, trumps to the right and other suits ranked in rows, as soon as the first card is played, and this player takes no further active part in the hand. The defending player to the declarer's left leads, followed by the other players clockwise round the table. The dealer plays a card from the dummy hand followed by one from his own hand after the opponent to his right has laid a card. Players must follow suit unless unable to do so, in which case a card from another suit, or a trump, may be played. The highest card of the suit led, or the highest trump, wins the trick.

CONCLUSION

Winning a game in bridge does not mean the contest is over. Game is awarded to a partnership that amasses 100 points or more below the line (either in a single contract or by adding together the scores of two or more). Partnerships must then score again from scratch in another game. The first partnership to win two out of the three games takes the rubber.

PARTNERSHIP BRIDGE VARIANTS

Various forms of Bridge have developed over the years, including Duplicate Bridge, the game normally played in clubs, tournaments and competitions, Chicago Bridge, where a game is completed in four deal; and Auction Bridge, the precursor of Contract Bridge. Although the rules of bidding and play are the same in Auction and Contract Bridge, the scoring system is different.

AUCTION BRIDGE

In Auction Bridge, the notion of vulnerability does not exist, so there is no extra penalty for failing to fulfil a contract if your partnership has won a game already. Odd tricks – that is, tricks over the book – are scored below rather than above the line and count towards winning a game.

Clubs count for six points, Diamonds seven, Hearts eight and Spades nine. If the contract is doubled, so is the number of points. If it is redoubled, Clubs are worth 24 points, Diamonds 28, Hearts 32 and Spades 36. Undertricks are scored above the line, as are bonuses for completing the contract and making a Grand or Small Slam. The first partnership to score 30 points below the line wins that game and the first one to win two games takes the rubber, and is awarded another 250 bonus points.

CHICAGO BRIDGE

The advantage of Chicago Bridge is that it is complete in four contracts. Vulnerability (whereby a side, having won a game towards the rubber, is subject to increased scores or penalties) varies from hand to hand in a fixed pattern. In the first hand, neither partnership is vulnerable. In the second, North and South are vulnerable; and in the third, East and West are vulnerable. In the final hand, both partnerships are vulnerable.

To determine the score for a successful contract, players first work out the score for the number of tricks made, including overtricks and taking any doubling into account. If the value of the contract was less than 100 points, 50 points are added for a part-score. If it was more than 100, 300 points are added if the partnership is not vulnerable; 500 are added if it is. The score for defeating a contract is the same as in Contract Bridge. There is no score for honours, nor extras for the rubber.

At the end of the fourth and deciding deal, if either side has a part-score – that is, points greater than zero but less than the magic 100 below the line – it receives a bonus of 100 points above the line.

VARIANTS

In Rubber Bridge, each hand is freshly dealt at random, and scores depend as much on the run of the cards as on the skills of the players.

In Duplicate Bridge, rather than trying to win more points than the opposing partnership, the aim is to do better than others playing the same cards. Each partnership is known as a pair and the final scores are calculated by comparing each pair's result with those of the others playing the same hand. Special four-way card holders called bridge boards are used to pass each player's hand to the next table to play it, while so-called bidding boxes, invented in Sweden in the 1960s, are also often used. At times, players are split into teams of four.

Other forms of Bridge include Reverse Bridge, where all cards rank back to front (in other words, Twos are the highest cards, followed by Threes, Fours and so on down to Aces, which are the lowest); Nullo Bridge, in which partnerships bid to lose tricks rather than to win them, and Brint, a variant of Bridge devised in the late 1920s, which is distinguished by its extremely elaborate – some would say over-sophisticated – scoring system. Basically, the higher the bid, the more each trick is worth. These three Bridge variants are rarely played.

Left: Bidding boxes carry a set of cards, each bearing the name of a legal call in Bridge. This allows the player to make a call by displaying the appropriate card from the box, rather than speaking aloud and chancing others hearing the bid.

PIRATE BRIDGE

This type of Bridge certainly seems to be a contradiction in terms, since, instead of playing in fixed partnerships, players switch alliances between deals.

Bridge authorities claim that Pirate Bridge was developed by R. F. Foster in 1917, but it seems likely that the occultist Aleister Crowley (1875–1947) devised it and Foster put the rules into definite shape. Crowley thought that what he had devised was 'such an improvement on the ordinary game', but it suffers from the fact that players with the best-matched hands inevitably manage to identify each other and make their contract easily as a result.

Pirate replaces fixed partnerships by floating alliances made from deal to deal. The dealer is the first to bid. Each player in turn has the choice of whether to accept the bid, so signalling his willingness to become dummy in partnership with the bidder, or passing. If all players pass, the hands are thrown in and the deal starts again. The player to the left of the previous bidder takes up the bidding. If the bid is accepted, each player in turn from the acceptor's left around the table may bid higher, pass, double or, if a double has been bid, redouble. If all players pass, the bid becomes the contract. A player may choose to make a new bid, which can be accepted or rejected by the previous bidder or acceptor. The latter can also try to break an alliance by naming a new contract when it is his turn to play, but, if no higher bid is accepted, that alliance must stand.

A double reopens the bidding. Making this bid gives sometime allies the chance to bid themselves out of their alliance by naming another bid in the hopes that another player will accept it. Or, if they are sufficiently confident, they can choose to redouble the accepted bid.

Once the contract is established, the declarer leads the opening trick, his partner laying down his hand as dummy. Play then proceeds in strict rotation around the table, even if declarer and dummy are seated next to rather than opposite one another. Scores are recorded below or above the line for each player. The game is scored in the conventional way (see scores at Contract Bridge), with individual scores noted above or below the line by each player involved.

Above: Aleister Crowley, occultist and probable inventor of Pirate Bridge.

THREE-HANDED BRIDGE

Aficionados of Bridge have ways of playing, even without the regulation four players. Three-Handed Bridge has many devotees, particularly to the following two games.

CUT-THROAT BRIDGE

In this simple version of Three-Handed Bridge, the dealer deals four hands, leaving one hand face down on the card table to eventually form the dummy. The declarer is the person who bids the highest. He turns the dummy face up between the two defenders after the left-hand opponent has led. Alternatively, players can mutually agree to turn one or more of the dummy cards face up after each bid.

TOWIE AND BOOBY

In Towie, a three-handed variant that two American players devised in 1931, six of the dummy cards are dealt face up. The highest bidder becomes the declarer, turning up and playing the whole of the dummy hand.

In Booby, each player is dealt 17 cards, with one extra card being dealt face down. Each makes four discards face down to complete the dummy. Bidding follows the conventional pattern, with the addition of a *Nullo* bid. Ranking between Hearts and Spades, this is a bid to lose a specified number of tricks, playing at No Trump. A bid of two *Nullos* is a bid to win no more than five tricks, while seven *Nullos* corresponds to a *Misère*, i.e. losing all tricks. *Nullo* bids are valued at 30 points per trick.

WHIST

Whist was the game of choice for many serious card players until Bridge took over from it in the early 20th century. Its popularity dates from the mid-1700s, when Edmond Hoyle described it in the first-ever rulebook of card games that was published in 1746. There is no bidding in classic Whist, but there are sufficient nuances in the play to make it a fascinating game.

OBJECT

To win as many of the 13 tricks as possible.

CONVENTIONS

Like Bridge, Whist has its own accepted conventions, or 'conventional leads' as they are strictly termed, worked out when the game was most in vogue. These have been

| **You will need:** 52 cards; no Jokers; scorecards |
| **Card ranking:** Standard, Aces high |
| **Players:** Four, in partnerships sitting opposite each other |
| **Ideal for:** 10+ |

condensed and simplified in the table below. Leading to the first trick gives the player the advantage of setting the pace and being able to make the best use of the cards in hand to try to signal to a partner which cards are held. This signal is used if the player concerned does not hold the Ace or King of that suit.

Conventions include finessing (playing the third highest card of a suit while also holding the highest, to draw out opponents' highest cards); leading with a trump (to indicate that you are holding five or more in your hand), and forcing (leading with a suit you believe one of the other players does not hold).

THE RULE OF ELEVEN

A further convention – leading the fourth best of your longest suit (counting from the top down), enables a player to apply what is termed the 'rule of eleven' to gauge the lie of the cards. Assuming your partner has led his fourth highest card, you subtract its face value from 11, to establish (in theory), how many of the higher cards are lacking from his hand. By further subtracting the number you hold yourself, you can deduce the number of higher cards held by the opposing side.

To show that he is holding an Ace, for instance, a player will lead a King. If a player leads the Seven of a suit in which his partner holds the Jack and King, this means that there are four cards above the Seven against him, of which his partner holds two. The partner cannot hold the Ace, or he would have played it, so his hand must include any four cards from Queen and Ten down to Seven, while the opposing partnership must hold the Ace and any one of Queen, Ten, Nine and Eight between them.

REVOKES

If a player does not follow suit when able to do so, a penalty is imposed. The cost of this (known as a revoke) is three game points, which can either be added to the opponents' score or subtracted from that of the revoking partnership. If both partnerships revoke, the hand is abandoned and a new one dealt.

CONVENTIONS

In plain suits

When holding	1st lead		2nd lead
• A, K, Q, J	K	then	J
• A, K, Q	K	then	Q
• A, K–J	K	then	A
• A, K	A	then	K
• K, Q, J, x	K	then	J
• K, Q, J, x, x	J	then	K
• K, Q, J, x, x and more	J	then	Q
• A, x, x, x, x and more	A	then	4th highest of remainder
• K, Q, x and more	K	then	4th highest of remainder
• A, Q, J	A	then	Q
• A, Q, J, x	A	then	Q
• A, Q, J, x, x	A	then	J
• K, J, 10, 9	9	then	K (if A or Q fails)
• Q, J, x	Q		
• Q, J, x, x and more	4th highest		

In trump suits

When holding	1st lead		2nd lead
• A, K, Q, J	J	then	Q
• A, K, Q	Q	then	K
• A, K, x, x, x, x and more	K	then	A
• A, K, x, x, x, x	4th highest		

PLAYER C

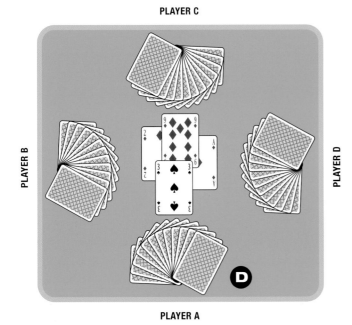

PLAYER B

PLAYER D

PLAYER A

Above: With Diamonds having been played by Player B, Players C and D follow suit. The A♦ seems set to win the trick, but Player A is out of Diamonds, so wins the trick with a low trump.

THE DEAL

Who deals first is determined by cutting the pack. The player to the dealer's left shuffles and the one to the right cuts the cards before the deal is made. Each player is singly dealt 13 cards face down except for the last card, which is turned up to denote trumps for that hand. The dealer claims the card when the trick is led. Otherwise, players can agree trumps in advance, in which case the convention is to follow a fixed sequence: Hearts, Diamonds, Spades and Clubs. No Trumps can also be introduced, so every fifth hand is played without trumps. Subsequent deals pass clockwise to the next player, who shuffles as before.

PLAY

Play starts with the person seated to the dealer's left, moving clockwise around the table. The first card becomes the suit for the trick. The other players must follow suit if they can. If they cannot, they can play a trump or discard any card. The player playing the highest card of the suit that has been led or the highest trump, if any are played, takes the trick. To claim it, he turns it face down in front of him. The winner leads play for the next trick.

Right: Player D, the first to lead, played the K♠, indicating that he also holds the A♠. His partner, Player B, lays the Q♠, almost certainly indicating he holds either a singleton (just one card) or doubleton (just two cards) in Spades.

SCORING

The partnership that gets to or exceeds five game points first – seven game points in the USA – wins the game. A rubber is a match that consists typically of three games, and is therefore won by the first side to win two. The match is won by the partnership with the highest number of game points at the end of the rubber.

In a five-point game, points can be won from tricks, honours and revokes. The first six tricks do not score, while tricks from seven to 13 are worth one game point each. If a partnership holds all the honour cards, the Ace, King, Queen and Jack of trumps, it gains four game points. If three honour cards are held, two extra game points are given. The winning partnership is also given a game point if its opponents make three or four tricks, two points if they make only one or two, and three points if they fail to score at all. In the seven-point system, players who revoke concede two game points to the opposing partnership. The final score is the difference between seven and the number of game points, if any, won by the losers. The final hand is played even after seven points have been won, and the points are added to the final score.

CONCLUSION

The game continues until all 13 tricks have been won. If one partnership takes all tricks, it is termed a Slam.

PLAYER C

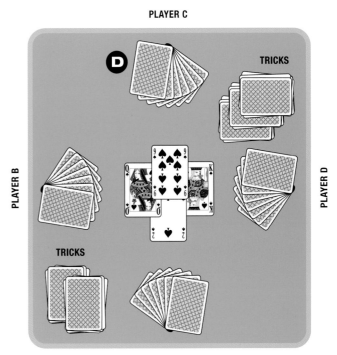

TRICKS

PLAYER B

PLAYER D

TRICKS

TRICKS

PLAYER A

BID WHIST

Many other games have developed from Whist, often with some element of bidding added. Perhaps the most significant of these is Bid Whist, which is widely played by the African-American community in the USA. Other interesting bidding variants include Norwegian Whist, in which the aim can be to lose tricks rather than win them, and Contract Whist, which is much like Bridge but without the dummy.

OBJECT

To fulfil the contract as bid and so score the points that are necessary to win the game.

THE DEAL

The player who draws the first Diamond deals first. Each player is dealt 12 cards, the remaining six being placed face down on the table to form a kitty.

TAKING THE KITTY

What happens after the deal depends on whether trumps are being played. If they are played, the successful bidder 'sports' the kitty, turning it up so the cards can be seen, and adds it to his hand before discarding six cards. Once sported in this way, the kitty counts as the first book to be won by the partnership. If there are No Trumps, the kitty is not shown to the other players.

You will need: 52 cards plus two Jokers, marked (or differentiated) the 'Big' Joker and the 'Little' Joker; scorecards

Card ranking: In high bids ('uptown'), cards rank Ace down to Two. In low bids ('downtown'), cards rank Ace up to King. In trump bids, cards rank Big Joker, Little Joker, Ace down to Two (uptown) or up to King (downtown)

Players: Four in partnerships, sitting opposite each other

Ideal for: 14+

BIDDING

Each player can bid only once, or pass. Each bid must be higher than the last. If the first three players pass, the dealer must bid. A bid consists of a number from three to seven, indicating the number of tricks (called 'books') above six that the bidder's team contracts to make.

Adding 'uptown' to a bid means that a trump suit will be named once the bidding is over and that high cards will win, while adding 'downtown' means that low cards will. When bidding No Trumps, a player waits until the end of bidding before specifying whether high or low cards count for more.

PLAY

Any card may be led, players following suit if possible. If not, they can play a trump or a card from a different suit. The ranking of the cards depends on what has been specified in the bid. If a player fails to follow suit despite holding an appropriate card, this is a renege and the reneging side is penalized. If it has won enough books, three are taken away from it. If not, the non-reneging team is deemed to have won 13 books.

SCORING AND CONCLUSION

Players score points by bidding for and winning books. A game consists of 13 books, and each book won above six is worth a point, but, in order to score, the bidding side must make at least as many points as it has bid. If it fails, the points that were bid are subtracted from the score. If the winning bid is No Trumps, scores are doubled. Winning all 13 books is termed a 'Boston', in which case, scores are quadrupled. The game continues until all 13 tricks have been won.

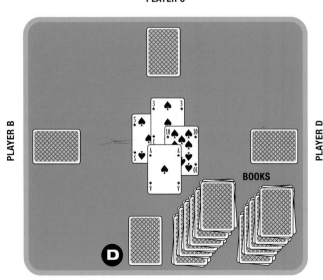

PLAYER C

PLAYER B

PLAYER D

BOOKS

PLAYER A

Left: This trick takes the A–C partnership to 12 tricks (or books, as they are called in Bid Whist). If they can win the last trick, they will have made a 'Boston', in which case, scores are quadrupled.

SPADES

Devised in the USA during the 1930s, Spades came of age globally with the coming of the Internet and the mushrooming of online card rooms. It is a plain-trick game (that is, one in which the winner or loser is determined solely by the number of tricks scored) in which Spades are always trumps. There are numerous variations in the rules, but what follows is the most generally accepted one.

OBJECT

To win at least as many tricks as bid for, or no tricks at all.

THE DEAL

The first dealer is chosen at random, after which the deal rotates clockwise. The cards are dealt singly, starting with the player to the dealer's left. Each player receives a total of 13 cards.

BIDDING

Players contract to win a specified number of tricks, the non-dealer partnership declaring first. Each pair's bids are added, the total being the number of tricks that

You will need: 52-card deck; scorecards

Card ranking: Standard, Aces high

Players: Usually four, in fixed partnerships of two, although it can be adapted to suit two, three or six players

Ideal for: 10+

Left: The lowest and highest trumps in Spades. The A♠ will always win whatever trick it is laid to, while the 2♠ will win only when used to trump and no higher Spade is played to the trick.

partnership must win in order to make the contract. Once made, bids cannot be changed. Nor are players allowed to pass, although a player who believes that he can lose every trick may declare 'nil'. If that is the case, his partner must state how many tricks he is prepared to win.

PLAY

The player to the dealer's left leads. Any card, except a Spade, can be led, and other players must follow suit if they can. Some versions of the game stipulate that players must lead their lowest Club on the first trick and that anyone void in Clubs must discard a Diamond or a Heart.

Spades may not be played until either a player plays one because he cannot follow suit – this is known as 'breaking Spades' – or until the leader has nothing but Spades left. If no Spades are played, the player of the highest card of the suit that has been led wins the trick. Otherwise, the highest Spade wins.

SCORING AND CONCLUSION

The side scoring 500 points first wins the game. Taking at least as many tricks as were bid means that the bidding partnership scores 10 times what it bid, and an extra point for each overtrick. These overtricks are known as 'bags'.

If a nil bid succeeds, the bidding players' side scores an extra 50 points, which are added to the score his partner makes for tricks taken. If the bid is unsuccessful, the partnership forfeits 50 points, but any tricks taken by the unsuccessful bidder count towards fulfilling their partner's contract. The game continues until all 13 tricks have been won.

PLAYER C

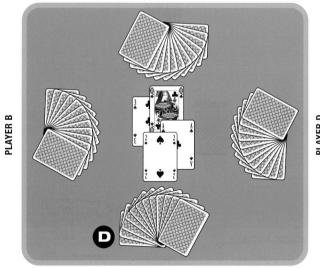

PLAYER B

PLAYER D

PLAYER A

Above: Some versions of Spades stipulate that players must lead their lowest Club, as here. Surprisingly, the last player to play has won the trick with the 2♠, meaning that he must be void in Clubs. Laying the first spade like this is known as 'breaking Spades'.

KAISER

Although Kaiser is German for 'emperor', this intriguing trick-taking game did not originate in Germany. Ukrainian immigrants to Canada are thought to have developed it half a century or so ago, although whether they brought it over from their homeland or devised it for themselves is a mystery. The side that bids highest chooses the trump suit, unless playing No Trumps.

OBJECT

To win at least as many tricks as bid, or to bring down the opposing partnership's bid.

THE DEAL

The deal and play are both clockwise. The first dealer is chosen at random, with the deal passing to the left after each hand. All the cards in the pack are dealt singly, so that each player ends up with a hand of eight cards.

BIDDING

Once the deal has been completed, each player, starting with the player to the dealer's left, has one chance to bid or to pass. The possible bids are from five to 12 points.

You will need: 32 cards including Sevens to Aces, but with the 3♠ replacing 7♠ and 5♥ replacing 7♥; scorecards

Card ranking: Standard, Aces high

Players: Four, in partnerships of two

Ideal for: 14+

Each must be higher than the one before it, although the dealer only needs to equal the highest bid to win the bidding. It is unnecessary to specify a trump suit in a bid, but a player who wants to play No Trumps must say so. If all the players pass, the hands are thrown in and the deal passes to the next player.

PLAY

The highest bidder chooses trumps and leads to the first trick, the other players following suit if possible, or playing any other card. The trick is taken by the player of the highest card of the suit that has been led, or by the player of the highest trump, if trumps are being played.

SCORING AND CONCLUSION

When all the cards have been played, the tricks are counted and scored. Each team gets one point for each trick it takes, plus five points for winning a trick containing the 5♥.

If it wins a trick containing the 3♠, it loses three points. If the side that chose trumps makes as many points as it bid, it adds that number of points to the score. If it took fewer, the bid is subtracted. If No Trumps was played, the figures are doubled.

If the bidding team's opponents have a cumulative score of less than 45 points, they score what they took. If it is 45 or more, the score is pegged, unless they end up with a negative score. In that case, the points are deducted from their total. Fifty-two points are needed to win the game.

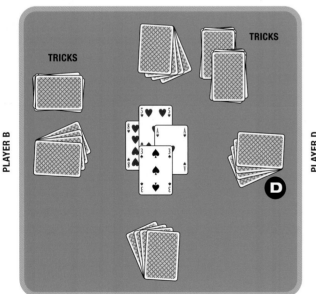

PLAYER C

TRICKS

TRICKS

PLAYER B

PLAYER D

PLAYER A

Above: Player C here looks to be on target to score a five-point bonus for his partnership by winning a trick containing the 5♥. However, Player A, unable to follow suit, plays the 3♠, thus reducing the trick's value to three points (one for the trick, plus five for the 5♥, minus three for the 3♠).

Left: Winning a trick containing the 5♥ scores the player concerned an extra five points. One containing the 3♠ loses three points.

FORTY-ONE

This game originated in the Middle East, where it is a favourite among Syrian and Lebanese card players. Players partner each other as in Bridge; North and South play against East and West. Hearts is the permanent trump suit.

You will need: 52-card deck; no Jokers; scorecards

Card ranking: Standard, Aces high

Players: Four, in partnerships of two

Ideal for: 14+

OBJECT

For one member of a partnership to win 41 points or more, and for all players to retain a positive score. A running total score is kept for each individual player.

THE DEAL

Each player gets 13 cards, dealt anti-clockwise around the table. The deal also rotates anti-clockwise. The first card is dealt singly, but others are dealt in twos.

Right: Forty-One is a much played card game in Syria, and to some extent in Lebanon. Even though it is a parnership game, a running total score is kept for each individual player.

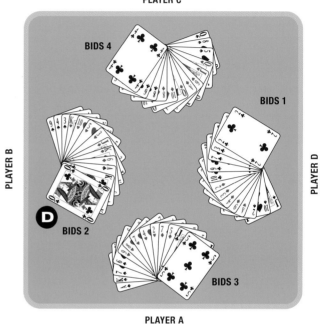

PLAYER C

BIDS 4

BIDS 1

PLAYER B

PLAYER D

D BIDS 2

BIDS 3

PLAYER A

Above: The bidding shows that Player A aims to make three tricks, Player B two, Player C four and Player D one. As this falls one short of the minimum 11 tricks needed, the hands must be thrown in and the cards dealt again.

BIDDING

The bidding starts with the player to the right of the dealer. Each player gets one chance to bid, stating the minimum number of tricks he expects to make. When added up, the bids must reach a minimum total of 11. Otherwise, the hands are thrown in and there is a new deal.

Bids of one to six score a point per trick if successful, otherwise they lose one point per trick. Bids of seven or more win or lose two points per trick bid. The common practice is to bid between two and six tricks. The dealer then decides whether to play the hand or not, and can bid to take the total up to the 11 needed for play to commence or he can over or under bid for a new deal.

PLAY

The player seated to the dealer's right leads. Any card of any suit may be led, but subsequent play must follow suit if possible. If not, a player can discard from another suit or trump with a Heart. If no trump is played, the highest card of the suit that has been led wins the trick. Otherwise, the highest Heart played wins. The winner of each trick then leads to the next.

SCORING AND CONCLUSION

Each player's score is recorded cumulatively. A player who takes as many tricks as he bid scores the value of the bid. There is no bonus for taking tricks over and above the bid. A player who bids and takes seven or more tricks scores twice the number of tricks bid. If that player fails to take enough tricks in a subsequent hand, he loses the doubled points, i.e. 14. This can be important. Although it is only one player who has to reach the magic total of 41 points or more, the partnership can win the game only if the other partner's cumulative score is positive rather than negative. Play continues until all 13 tricks have been won.

VINT

This game originated in Tsarist Russia. It is thought to be an ancestor of Bridge, although there is no dummy and the tricks taken by both partnerships count towards a game. Vint in Russian means 'screw', which alludes to the way in which players force bids up by outbidding each other in the first of the two auctions that start off the game.

OBJECT

To make as many tricks as bid for and to score 60 below the line for game. The first partnership to win two games scores a bonus of 400 points, the winners of the remaining four deals scoring 600, 800, 1,000 and 1,200 points, respectively.

THE DEAL

After the players have cut, the pack is dealt out to each player one card at a time.

BIDDING

The dealer begins the bidding. A bid is the number of tricks a player aims to take above six. A suit must be specified. If a player's bid is overcalled, he can make a higher one in the next bidding round, even at the expense of a partner.

The highest bidder becomes the declarer and starts the second auction, which ends when both partners have passed twice. The suit named in the highest-ranking bid becomes trumps unless the winning bid is No Trumps.

PLAY

The declarer leads, with each of the other players following with a card of the same suit. If a player cannot follow suit, he can play a trump or discard. The winner of the trick leads the next one.

Below and Right: Three Aces, or a same-suited sequence of three, is termed a coronet and scores 500 points. If the sequence is in the trump suit, it is termed a doubled coronet and scores 1,000 points.

You will need: 52 cards; no Jokers; scorecards
Card ranking: Standard, Aces high
Players: Four, in partnerships of two
Ideal for: 14+

Scores are recorded above and below the line, but the scorecard is split into four columns as opposed to two. The higher the bid, the more each trick is worth, with both partnerships scoring for the value of the tricks they take. On a bid of one, a trick is worth 10 points, on a bid of seven, it is 70 points. The total score is termed the game score and is entered below the line. Once a partnership scores 500 below-the-line points, the game is over.

SCORING AND CONCLUSION

All undertricks – tricks fewer than the numbers bid – incur a penalty of 100 times the trick value, entered above the line as a minus score. So, too, are bonus points for winning a game, rubber, Grand Slam (every trick) or Little Slam (every trick bar one), and honour points, which, in Vint, are the four Aces and top five trumps – there are nine in all, since the Ace of trumps counts twice.

They can be scored by either partnership, regardless of winning or losing, but whichever one holds the majority of them scores the number held multiplied by 10 times the value of the contract. For example, assuming that the contract is five, a partnership holding the Ace of trumps, two other Aces, and the King, Queen and Ten of trumps between them scores for the seven honours and five for the contract. They multiply this total by 10, so ending up with a score of 350 points. In No Trumps, they score 25 times the trick value.

If a player holds three Aces or a same-suited sequence of three, he scores 500 points, known as a coronet. If the sequence is in trumps, the score is doubled, and this is known as a doubled coronet. Play continues until all 13 tricks have been won.

QUINTO

In the early 1900s, Angelo John Lewis, better known as the stage magician 'Professor Hoffman', invented this imaginative variant of Whist. Quinto derives its name from the 'quints' that feature in the game – that is, the Joker, the Five of each suit, and two cards of the same suit totalling five. Points are gained for winning tricks, and especially for any quints that they may contain.

OBJECT

The object of the game is to score 250 points in as many deals as it takes.

THE DEAL

Each player is dealt 12 card singly, the remaining five being left face down on the table. Hoffman re-ferred to these as the 'cachette'.

Above: Also known as the Quint Royal, the Joker has no trick-taking value. However, it is worth 25 points to the partnership that wins it.

BIDDING

Once the cards have been dealt, and before play begins, each player has the opportunity to pass, double or redouble an opponent's double. Doubling, as the name suggests, doubles the value of each trick won from 5 to 10 points, while redoubling raises it still further to 20 points. If this happens, the relative value of quints to tricks is reduced. Quints can be the Joker, which is worth 25 points, the Five of each

Left: This trick would be worth 20 points: 10 points for the 2♣ and 3♣ (making a quint in Clubs) and another 10 for the 5♣ (another quint). The points are scored immediately after the trick is taken.

Left: This trick also has two quints within it: the 5♥ as well as the 4♥ and A♥. Here, though, because the suit is Hearts, each quint would score 20 points, making 40 points in total.

You will need: 52-card deck; one Joker; scorecards

Card ranking: Standard, with suits also ranked, Spades (lowest), Clubs, Diamonds, Hearts (highest)

Players: Four, in partnerships of two

Ideal for: 14+

suit or two cards of the same suit totalling five in the same trick. A quint in Spades is worth five points, Clubs 10, Diamonds 15 and Hearts 20.

PLAY

Play starts with the player to dealer's left, partnerships competing to win tricks containing quints. The winner of a trick leads to the next. If possible, players have to follow suit, although if they cannot, they can play any card from their hands.

The game is played without trumps. The suits, however, are ranked, from low to high, starting with Spades followed by Clubs, Diamonds and Hearts. A player may discard from a lower suit if unable to follow the suit led. Equally, he may win the trick by playing a card from a higher suit. This inevitably means that the highest card of the highest suit played takes the trick. A player whose hand contains the Joker at the 11th trick must play it if the only other option is to win the trick.

SCORING

Each trick is worth five points, with bonuses for any quints in it. The top-scoring quint is the Joker – the Quint Royal. It is worth 25 points. It cannot be led to a trick, nor can it win a trick, but otherwise it may be played at any time. If a partnership wins a trick with a quint in it, it scores the quint immediately. Its value depends on its suit.

CONCLUSION

If scoring a quint means that the partnership has reached the 250-point target, play stops. If not, the side taking the final trick also wins the *cachette*, which counts as a 13th trick and scores for any quint or quints it may contain. All the tricks are then scored to ascertain if there is a winner. If not, or if the two sides are tied, there is a new deal.

WIDOW WHIST WHIST FOR THREE PLAYERS

Whist is flexible enough to be adapted to suit three or even two players. This classic version of Three-handed Whist is aptly termed Widow Whist. It gets its name from the extra hand that is dealt just to the left of the dealer. This is the widow, which players are given the chance to play rather than their own hands. In Widow Whist, Clubs are always trumps and each player is out for himself – there are no partnerships.

You will need: 52 cards; no Jokers; scorecards	
Card ranking: Standard, Aces high	
Players: Three	
Ideal for: 10+	

OBJECT

To win as many tricks as possible by playing the highest card of the suit led, or the highest trump.

THE DEAL

To establish who deals first, the players cut the deck for the highest card. The dealer then deals 13 cards each to the active players plus 13 cards face up for the widow.

PLAY

The player to the left of the dealer has first choice of playing the widow rather than his hand. If he decides not to play the widow, it is passed to the next person on the left, and so on, around the table. If a player takes the widow, the original hand is passed on.

SCORING AND CONCLUSION

If the player to the dealer's left decides to play the widow, he has to take only three tricks to break even – in other words, a point is awarded for every trick taken over three. Any other player taking the widow has to take four tricks before he starts scoring. Play continues until all 13 tricks have been won.

GERMAN WHIST WHIST FOR TWO PLAYERS

Two-handed versions of Whist include German Whist, in which players start with either 13 or six cards each. Despite the name, the game is thought to have originated in Britain.

You will need: 52 cards; no Jokers; scorecards	
Card ranking: Standard, Aces high	
Players: Two	
Ideal for: 7+	

OBJECT

To win high-ranking cards in the first phase of the game in order to win the majority of the tricks in the second.

THE DEAL

Thirteen cards are dealt to each player; the remaining cards are placed face down on the table to form the stock. The top card of the stock is turned up for trumps.

PLAY

The non-dealer leads and the dealer must follow suit. If unable, he may discard any card or play a trump. The highest card of the suit led wins the trick unless it is trumped. The trick's winner picks up the face-up card from the top of the stock and adds it to his hand. The loser takes the next face-down card. The trick's winner leads, turning up the top card of the stock. Players aim to add as many good cards from the stock to their hand as they can, which means they try to win tricks only if they think that the exposed card on top of the stock is likely to be worth more than the one beneath. Once the stock is exhausted, the two players aim to win the majority of the remaining 13 tricks.

SCORING AND CONCLUSION

The only tricks to score are those won in the second phase of the game, after the stock has run out. Whoever wins the most tricks (seven or over) wins the game, or, if a succession of games are being played, the difference between the two totals at the end of the last trick. Play ends when all of the final 13 tricks have been won.

CALYPSO

Invented in the West Indies in the early 1950s, this is a partnership game in which each player uses the cards he wins to form 'calypsos' – all 13 cards of a given suit. Who partners whom is established by cutting the deck. Players with the highest cards partner each other against the ones with the lowest. Whoever cuts highest of all becomes the dealer and chooses where to sit, thus determining his own and the other players' personal trumps. In Calypso, North's trumps are always Hearts, South's are Spades, East's are Diamonds and West's are Clubs.

OBJECT

To build calypsos – all 13 cards of a given suit – in one's own trump suit, to help one's partner build his own, and to hinder the opposing partnership's attempts at calypso building.

THE DEAL

The player who cut the highest, deals first. There are four deals in all, one by each player. Each player is dealt 13 cards singly, the rest of the pack (containing all four packs shuffled together) being placed face down to one side of the table. These cards are gradually used up in subsequent deals.

PLAY

Tricks are played for, with players following suit where possible. If not, they can discard, or trump each trick using their personal trump suit. The only cards that can be used to construct a calypso are those won in tricks. Each calypso must be complete before a player can start building another, the process being made harder by the fact that any cards within a trick that duplicate ones already in a calypso cannot be retained for building any future calypsos.

The player who wins a trick takes the cards he needs from it and hands over any his partner requires. The remaining cards – those played by the opposing partnership and those unusable cards from the winning partnership's hands – are stacked face down in a winnings pile. When complete, the calypso is laid face up in front of the player who made it.

You will need: Four 52-card decks; scorecards
Card ranking: Standard, Aces high
Players: Four, in partnerships of two
Ideal for: 10+

SCORING

Each partnership scores points as follows:
- 500 for each partnership's first calypso.
- 750 for each partnership's second calypso.
- 1,000 for each partnership's subsequent calypsos.
- 20 per card in an unfinished calypso.
- 50 for each card in the winnings pile.

Above: South has just laid down a calypso in the appropriate personal trump suit (Spades) and led to a new trick. West seemed on course to win this, until North laid a personal trump, only to be trumped again by East, whose personal trump suit is Diamonds.

CONCLUSION

After 13 tricks have been taken, the deal passes to the player to the left of the previous dealer and new hands are then dealt. The procedure continues until four deals have been completed, after which the game is scored.

2 | QUICK-TRICK GAMES

WHAT DISTINGUISHES MOST QUICK-TRICK GAMES IS THAT NOT ALL THE CARDS ARE DEALT OUT, THUS MAKING IT HARD FOR PLAYERS TO DEDUCE WHAT THEIR OPPONENTS ARE HOLDING. THE GAMES RANGE FROM SOPHISTICATED ONES WITH AN ESTABLISHED HISTORICAL PEDIGREE, REQUIRING AN ADVANCED LEVEL OF SKILL, SUCH AS EUCHRE, TO TRUC, A SPANISH AND PROVENÇAL GAME IN WHICH TRICKS ARE WON BY BLUFF RATHER THAN BY CALCULATION.

Most quick-trick card games involve gambling. In most of them, each player is dealt three cards, the aim being to win a single trick; or five cards, in which case he has to take at least three tricks; or bid a minimum number. Bidding is the hallmark of games of skill such as Euchre, Five Hundred and Napoleon (or Nap as it is more commonly known). In their day, all three games attracted a fanatical following.

Although it is French by origin, and thought to descend from a game called Juckerspiel that was formerly played in Alsace, Euchre was, at one time, the most popular trumps game in the USA. Originally brought to Pennsylvania by German immigrants known as the Pennsylvania Dutch, Euchre has the distinction of being the first game to use the Joker. This was introduced at some time during the 1850s, to serve as the highest trump. The Joker started to appear in the well-known guise of the court jester around 1880.

Above: This classic image of a jester playing a flute, with a ninny stick attached to his belt, appeared on cards around 1880.

The origins of Napoleon or Nap are particularly interesting. Some authors suggest that it derived its name from the French Emperor Napoleon III, the nephew of the great Napoleon, who popularized a version of it in the mid-19th century. Others trace its roots back even further, to the First French Empire (1804–14), pointing out that the names of Wellington and Blücher, Napoleon's successful adversaries at the Battle of Waterloo in 1815, feature in it as possible bids, as does Napoleon himself.

EUCHRE

This popular partnership game is played widely in Canada, the north-eastern USA and in England's West Country. Although the essentials are fairly consistent, the game has a wide range of variations. In North America, it is customary to play with a 24-card deck, but in British Euchre, a Joker, known as Benny or Best Bower, is added.

OBJECT

To win at least three of the five tricks, in which case the score is one point. If the same partnership takes all five tricks, they score two points.

CARD RANKING

Aces are the highest-ranking cards and Nines the least valuable ones, but there are two exceptions. The Joker (Benny or Best Bower) is the highest trump, followed by the Jack of the trump suit, the so-called Right Bower, and the other Jack of the same colour, which is the Left Bower.

THE DEAL

Each player is dealt five cards, the remaining cards being placed face down on the table. The dealer, chosen at random, turns the top card face up to set the trump suit.

BIDDING

Starting to the left of the dealer, players bid to establish which side will win at least three tricks with the face-up card's suit as trump. As soon as a player says, 'I accept', taking the face-up card and replacing it with one of his own face down, the bidding is over. The alternative is to pass. If everyone passes, a new bidding round ensues.

The partnership that chooses trumps is known as the 'makers' and the other as the 'defenders'. However, a player with a strong hand may bid to 'go alone' – that is, to play the hand without a partner. This means that the other player places his cards face down on the table and sits out the hand.

PLAY

The player to the dealer's left leads, unless someone has decided to go alone, in which case the lead passes to the player on that person's left. If two players go alone, the player of the team that did not choose trumps leads.

You will need: 24-card deck (Eights and below having been removed from a standard pack); one Joker; scorecards

Card ranking: See under 'Card Ranking' below

Players: Four, in partnerships of two

Ideal for: 14+

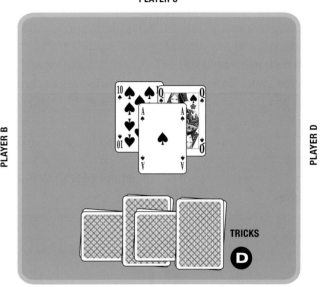

Above: Player A, going alone, wins the final trick, thus taking all five tricks (a March). His partnership scores five bonus points.

Players must follow suit if possible, otherwise they may play any card. The highest card played in the led suit wins the trick, unless trumps are played. If so, the highest trump wins, and the winner leads to the next trick.

SCORING

If all four players take part, the makers score a point for taking three or four tricks. If they take all five – termed a 'March' – they get a bonus point. If they fail to win three, they are 'euchred' and the defenders score two points.

If a maker goes alone and wins all five tricks, the partnership scores five points, or one point if the score is three or four tricks. If a defender does so and wins three or more tricks, that partnership scores four points.

CONCLUSION

The winning partnership is the first to score an agreed number of points (such as 10, 11 or 21).

PEPPER

The modern descendant of a game called *Hasenpfeffer* (Jugged Hare), this fast-paced game is closely related to Euchre. The chief differences are that, in Pepper, all the cards are dealt, and an element of bluffing is also encouraged. As in Euchre, the top trumps are the Right and Left Bowers (Jack of trumps and Jack of the same colour), but there is an additional No Trumps bid in which the Ace in every suit ranks the highest.

OBJECT

To make at least the number of tricks bid and to score 30 or more points. If both sides reach this total in the same hand, the result is a draw.

CARD RANKING

The Jack of the trump suit, the so-called Right Bower, is the highest trump, followed by the other Jack of the same colour (the Left Bower). Aces are the next highest-ranking cards and nines the least valuable. In a No Trump bid, cards rank Ace to Nine in all suits.

THE DEAL AND BIDDING

Six cards are dealt to each player singly, after which the player to the dealer's left bids, or passes, first. Players have one chance to bid, the choice being to pass or to

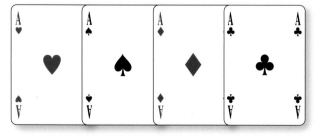

Above: As in Euchre, the Jack of trumps (here, it is Diamonds) is the top-ranking card and the other red Jack ranks second. The two Jacks are called the Right and Left Bowers, respectively. In a No Trumps contract, Aces are the highest cards, with Jacks ranking below Queens.

raise the bidding. Bids can be for one, two, three, four, or five tricks. The highest bids are Little Pepper and Big Pepper. Both are bids to take all six tricks, but the former is more conservative than the latter. A bid of Little Pepper means that the score for taking all six tricks is six. A bid of Big Pepper doubles the score to 12 points for winning all six tricks, but the penalty for failing to do so is also doubled.

PLAY

Players must follow suit, if possible, or otherwise play a trump or any card. The highest card of the suit led takes the trick, or the highest trump if trumps are played. The winner of each trick leads to the next.

SCORING AND CONCLUSION

The bidding side scores a point for each trick it takes if it makes its contract, but is set back (loses) six points if it fails. If the bid is Big Pepper, the bidders are set back 12 points. Their opponents score a point for each trick they take. The first partnership to score 30 or more points wins.

VARIANT

Some enthusiasts favour a different version of the game, in which the defenders can challenge or concede the hand at the end of bidding. If the decision is to challenge, actual play is restricted to the winner of the bidding and the two defenders, the remaining player sitting out the hand. If the defenders concede, the bidders score the value of the bid.

There is only one round of bidding, with the two highest bids becoming Pepper and Pepper Alone. They are worth seven and 14 points, respectively. Unless the bid is Pepper Alone, the successful partners exchange a card. Neither is allowed to look at the card until the exchange is completed. The main difference in the scoring system is that the defenders lose points if they fail to take any tricks, the amount varying with the bid's value, as do the penalties for not making the contract.

You will need: 24 card-deck (Twos to Eights having been removed from a standard pack); no Jokers; scorecards

Card ranking: See under 'Card Ranking' below

Players: Four, in partnerships of two

Ideal for: 10+

FIVE HUNDRED

Related to Euchre and Pepper, this fascinating game was originally devised and copyrighted by the United States Playing Card company in 1904. While still played in the USA, it has since become extremely popular in Australia and New Zealand.

OBJECT

To achieve a score of 500 points or more as a result of winning a contract.

CARD RANKING

The rank order for trumps is Joker, Right Bower (Jack of trumps), Left Bower (Jack of the same colour suit) and then Ace down to Seven. In No Trump hands, there are no Bowers. The Joker becomes the highest-ranking card in whatever suit is chosen by the player holding it and so will win any trick in which it is played.

THE DEAL

Who deals first is established by cutting the pack, Kings ranking highest, Aces second to lowest and the Joker the lowest. The player making the lowest cut wins the deal. Each player is dealt 10 cards in packets of three, two, three and two, or three, three, three and one. The three cards left over are placed face up to form a kitty.

BIDDING

Starting with the player to the dealer's left, each player bids in turn. The options are to name a contract with a higher value than the preceding one, or to pass. Each step upward in the bidding is termed a 'jump'.

When bidding, players must state how many tricks they expect to make, (the highest number that can be bid is 10 and the lowest six), and nominate trumps or

You will need: 32-card deck (Sixes and below having been removed from a standard pack); one Joker; scorecards

Card ranking: See under 'Card Ranking' below

Players: Three is optimal

Ideal for: 10+

Left: Although holding the Ace, this player's long suit in Spades makes this an excellent hand for bidding *Open Misère* – a contract played out with the declarer's cards face up on the table.

No Trumps. A No Trump bid ranks the highest, followed by one in Hearts, Diamonds, Clubs and Spades. This makes the most valuable contract 10 No Trumps and the least valuable one six Spades. If the bid is *Misère*, the contract is to lose every trick at No Trumps. An Open *Misère*, the same bid but with cards exposed, scores double.

PLAY

The winning bidder, the contractor, starts by picking up the kitty and discards three cards face down to take its place. He can discard any three cards, including the ones he has just picked up. What happens next depends on the nature of the contract. If it is *Misère* or Open *Misère*, the contractor's partner takes no part in play, simply putting his hand face down on the table. The contractor leads to the first trick. The other players must follow suit if they can or, if they cannot trump, must play any card. The highest trump or the highest card of the suit led takes the trick, its winner leading to the next.

SCORING AND CONCLUSION

If the bidder wins the contract, the score is the value of the bid. A contract of 10 No Trumps scores 520 points, while one of six Spades is worth 40 points. If the contract fails, its value is deducted from its bidder's score.

The opposing players score 10 points for every trick they take. At *Misère*, they score 10 for each trick taken by the bidder. If a player contracted to take eight tricks or fewer manages to win all 10, a Grand Slam, the bonus is 250 points, or double the value of the contract. Play continues until all 10 tricks have been taken.

SCORES FOR CONTRACT MADE					
	♠	♣	♦	♥	No Trumps
Six	40	60	80	100	120
Seven	140	160	180	200	220
Eight	240	260	280	300	320
Nine	340	360	380	400	420
Ten	440	460	480	500	520
No tricks/No trump	*Misère* 250		Open *Misère* 500		

ECARTÉ

This elegant two-hander, derived from a French 15th-century game called Triomphe, was once extremely popular in casinos, largely because onlookers placed sizeable side-bets on the outcome. It is fast, skilful and extremely enjoyable to play, despite a somewhat convoluted scoring system involving whether cards are exchanged or not after the deal.

OBJECT

To score five points in order to win a game.

THE DEAL

The deal alternates, and each player is dealt five cards in packets of three then two, or two then three. The remaining cards are placed face down on the table to form a stock, and the dealer turns the top card up to determine which suit will be trumps. If the card is a King, the dealer scores a point. If this takes his total from previous games to five points, he wins automatically and there is no actual play.

EXCHANGING OF CARDS

If the non-dealer believes that he can make at least three tricks, he leads to the first trick, or otherwise can 'propose' that both players exchange some of their cards. What happens next is for the dealer to decide: he can accept the proposal or refuse it. If the dealer accepts, the non-dealer, followed by the dealer, discards at least one card and draws the same number of replacement cards from the top of the stock.

If the dealer's decision is to refuse the proposal, the hand is played without any exchange of cards. However, the dealer is now obliged to take at least three tricks and a failure to do so is reflected in the scoring.

The process can continue until the non-dealer decides to lead, the dealer refuses a proposal, or the stock is exhausted, in which case play must start immediately with the non-dealer leading to the first trick. Neither player may discard more cards than remain in the stock and the trump card may not be taken in hand.

> **You will need:** 32 card-deck (Sixes and below having been removed from a standard pack); scorecards
>
> **Card ranking:** Kings highest, then Queens, Jacks and Aces down to Sevens
>
> **Players:** Two
>
> **Ideal for:** 14+

SHOWING THE KING

If either player holds the King of trumps, he may show it before play and score a point, provided that he has not already played some other card to the first trick.

PLAY

At the start, the non-dealer plays first. The other player must follow suit and win the trick if possible, either by leading a higher card of the same suit or by trumping a non-trump lead. If he can do neither, he can play any card. The winner of each trick leads to the next.

SCORING

Taking three or four tricks wins a point, while taking five, a 'Vole', wins two points. If the player who rejected an exchange fails to take three tricks with the hand he was originally dealt, two points go to the opponent. Further deals ensue until one player scores 5 points. At the end of a game, if one player ends up with only one or two points, the other wins a double stake, which becomes a treble if the loser's score is zero.

CONCLUSION

The first player to score five points wins a game.

Left: A strong Ecarté hand. With the top card (King) in two suits, and strong cards in the others, it is likely to win at least three tricks unless the opponent's hand is almost all trumps. A player with these cards would have no need to countenance exchanging cards.

Right: If either player holds the King of trumps, he may show it before play and score a point. If the turn-up after the deal is a King, the dealer scores a point.

TWENTY-FIVE

The national card game of Ireland, Twenty-Five was originally called Spoil Five or Five Fingers, since the aim is to prevent anyone from winning three of the five tricks played. It is descended from a game called Maw, reputedly the favourite of James VI of Scotland (later James I of England). What makes the game unique is its peculiar card ranking, although this is soon mastered with a little practice.

OBJECT

To win at least three tricks – better still, all five – and sweep the kitty, or to stop opposing players from doing so (known as 'spoil five').

> **You will need:** 52-card deck; no Jokers; gambling chips/counters
> **Card ranking:** See under 'Suits and Ranking' below
> **Players:** Five considered ideal, although can be two to ten
> **Ideal for:** 14+

SUITS AND RANKING

The game is always played with a trump suit, the highest trumps being the Five of trumps (Five Fingers), Jack of trumps, A♥, and Ace of trumps if a trump other than Hearts is being played. The remaining cards rank according to the colour of their suit. Hearts and Diamonds rank from King and Queen down to Two and Ace, while Spades and Clubs rank King, Queen, Jack, Ace and from Two to Ten.

THE DEAL

Each player starts with a total of 20 chips and puts one into the kitty. Players then cut for the deal: the one to cut the lowest wins. Starting with the player to the dealer's left, five cards are dealt face down to each player in packets of two and three. The remaining cards are stacked face down, the dealer turning the top one up to determine trumps.

If the turned-up card is an Ace, the dealer may pick it up and exchange it for any unwanted card in his hand. This is termed 'robbing the pack'. Similarly, if a player is dealt the Ace of trumps, he may declare it, then rob the pack, by taking the turn-up and discarding an unwanted card face down, before playing to the first trick.

PLAY

The player to the dealer's left leads. If the lead is a plain suit, the other players must follow suit or trump. If they cannot, they may discard. If trumps are led, the same ruling applies, unless the only trump a player holds is one of the top three – a Five or Jack of trumps or the Ace of Hearts. In this case, assuming that the trump that was led is lower in value, the player can choose to discard from another suit rather than play the trump.

CONCLUSION

A player taking the first three tricks can choose to take the kitty or 'jinx' – that is, try to win the two tricks that remain. If successful, as well as taking the kitty, each player pays the jinxer a chip. If not, the jinxer loses the kitty and the tricks are 'spoilt'. The same applies if no one takes three tricks: the kitty is carried forward to the next hand, each player raising it by one chip.

Above: In Twenty-Five, the highest-ranking trump (here, Diamonds) is the Five, known as Five Fingers. The Jack of trumps ranks next, followed by the A♥ and Ace of trumps if a trump other than Hearts is being played.

Right: Descended from a game called Maw, Twenty-Five was reputedly the favourite card game of James VI of Scotland.

AUCTION FORTY-FIVES

This variant of Twenty-Five is a Canadian favourite, the ranking of the cards, the way in which tricks are played and the right to renege being the same as in the Irish original. The difference is that a bidding element is introduced, in which bids are made in multiples of five up to 30 without a suit being declared. The winning bidder names trumps.

OBJECT

To win, as a partnership, the requisite number of tricks to score 120 and so take the game, or, if not, to prevent the opposing partnership from doing so.

SUITS AND CARD RANKING

The game is always played with a trump suit, the highest trumps being the Five of trumps (Five Fingers), Jack of trumps, A♥, and Ace of trumps if a trump other than Hearts is being played. The other cards rank according to the colour of their suit. Hearts and Diamonds rank from King and Queen down to Ace, while Spades and Clubs rank King, Queen, Jack, Ace and from Two to Ten.

PLAYER C

PLAYER B

PLAYER D

PLAYER A

Above: Once bidding is over and trumps have been declared, each player in turn, starting with the player to the dealer's left, can discard as many cards as he wishes from his hand. Before dealing the required number of replacements, the dealer has the option of 'robbing the pack' – that is, examining all the cards that have not been dealt and adding any he wants to his hand.

You will need: 52 cards; no Jokers; scorecard
Card ranking: See under 'Suits and Card Ranking' below
Players: Four to six, in partnerships of two (in alternating seats)
Ideal for: 14+

THE DEAL

Each player is dealt five cards in packets of three and two or two and three. Once bidding is over and trumps have been declared, each player in turn, again starting with the player to the dealer's left, may decide to discard as many cards as he wishes from his hand face down on the table. Before dealing the required number of replacements, the dealer has the option of 'robbing the pack' – that is, to examine all the cards that have not been dealt and pick out whichever ones he wants in his hand.

BIDDING

The bidding starts with the player to the dealer's left and continues clockwise around the table. Each player in turn may bid or pass, although the player who passes may not re-enter the bidding at a later stage. Each bid must be higher than the one that preceded it, although the dealer has the privilege of opting to say, 'I hold'. This means that the last bid is equalled. The next player to bid must therefore raise the bid or decide to pass.

PLAY

The player to the left of the winning bidder leads. If the lead is a plain suit, other players must follow suit or trump. If they cannot, they may discard. If trumps are led, the same rule applies, unless the only trump a player holds is one of the top three and ranked higher than the led trump. In this case, the player may discard from another suit.

SCORING AND CONCLUSION

Each trick taken scores five points, as does the highest trump in play. If the bidding partnership takes at least the amount of the bid, it scores all the tricks won, but, if not, the amount of the bid is deducted from the score. The other partnership always scores what it has taken in tricks. If a partnership bids and makes 30 (the maximum number of possible points in a hand) the score is doubled to 60. A partnership that has won 100 or more points is not allowed to bid less than 20. The game is over when a partnership reaches 120 points.

NAPOLEON

In spite of its name, this is a British card game, which was extremely popular in Victorian times. A straightforward trick-taking game, the convention is to play Nap, as it is usually known, for small stakes and settle up after each hand. Although usually played with a standard deck, some players prefer to strip out the low cards of each suit to increase the skill factor. A Joker can also be added, in which case it becomes the highest trump, or in *Mis* – a bid to take no tricks – the only trump.

OBJECT
To make at least the number of tricks bid or to stop another player from doing so.

THE DEAL
It is standard practice to shuffle the cards only at the start of a game and after a successful bid of five. Otherwise, they are simply cut by the player to the dealer's right before each deal. Each player is dealt five cards in packets of three and two or two and three. The deal passes to the left after each hand.

BIDDING
Each player bids to win a number of tricks if given the lead and choice of trumps, starting with the player to the dealer's left, moving clockwise round the table. There is only one round in which each player must bid higher than the last one, or pass. The lowest bid is two, which is worth two points, followed by three, which scores three, *Mis* (lose every trick), also worth three, four, worth four, and Nap, which is worth five. A Wellington is worth five for doubled stakes and, if a Blücher follows, this is redoubled. A Wellington can be bid only if another player has already bid Nap and a Blücher can only follow a Wellington.

PLAY
The highest bidder leads to the first trick. The suit of the card that is led automatically becomes trumps, except in a *Mis* if it has been agreed that the bid should be played at No Trumps. Players must follow suit, if possible, or trump or, otherwise, play any card. The highest card of the suit led, or the highest trump if any are played, takes the trick, the winner leading to the next.

You will need: 52-card deck (occasionally with lower ranks removed or a Joker added); gambling chips/counters

Card ranking: Standard, Aces high

Players: Four to five is best

Ideal for: 14+

Left: The author Jerome K. Jerome mentions Victorian favourite Penny Nap in his celebrated book *Three Men in a Boat*.

SCORING AND CONCLUSION
If the bidder is successful, each of the opposing players has to pay him the value of the bid. If the bidder wins insufficient tricks, or, in the case of *Mis*, takes any at all, he must pay each opponent the same amount that would have been won had the contract been successful.

In some games, the payments for Nap, Wellington and Blücher are doubled if they are won, but not if they are lost. The game continues until all tricks have been played.

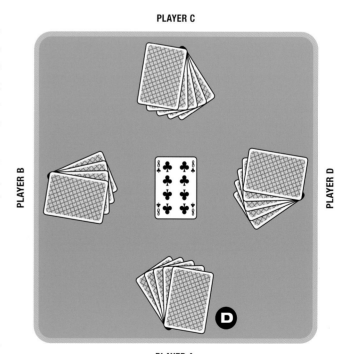

Above: Player B leads to the first trick, so Clubs automatically become trumps.

BRANDELN

This attractive game is the German equivalent of Nap. Its name in English means 'to smoulder'. Two of the bids – *Bettel* and *Herrenmord* – are for No Trump games. In the others, the successful bidder nominates trumps before he leads.

OBJECT

To take at least three tricks, the lowest possible bid, up to a maximum of seven. There is no bonus for overtricks.

BIDDING AND PLAY

Players are dealt seven cards. They may bid or pass. Each bid must be more than the previous one, unless an earlier bidder decides to 'hold' the bid of a later one, forcing that player to raise or pass. Bidding a *Brandeln* means taking three tricks and a score of a point. Four tricks wins two points, five wins three, and six wins four, while *Bettel*, (a *Mis* bid), *Mord* and *Herrenmord* score five, six and seven.

You will need: 28 card-deck (Eights, Sixes and below having been removed from a standard pack); scorecard

Card ranking: Ace, King, Queen, Jack, Ten, Nine, Seven in every suit except trumps (Jack, Seven, Ace, King, Queen, Ten, Nine)

Players: Four

Ideal for: 14+

The successful bidder announces trumps on leading to the first trick. The others must follow suit, trump or overtrump or otherwise play any card. The highest card of the suit led or the highest trump wins the trick. If successful, the bidder wins the value of the bid from each opponent; if unsuccessful, he deducts it from his score.

Left: In plain suits (left), card ranking is standard, Ace high. In the trump suit, (right, here ♣), the Jack and Seven are the top trumps.

RÖDSKÖGG

This is the Swedish version of Nap, the name of which translates as Redbeard. It is also known as Fem Opp (Five Up), probably because of the five-point penalties that feature in various stages of the game. It is played without trumps.

OBJECT

To shed enough points to end up with a score of zero from an opening score of 12.

THE DEAL

Players are each dealt six cards in two packets of three, after which the dealer 'knocks' with the words 'Knock for cards and misdeal'. Any player picking up his cards before the dealer knocks goes five up – that is, has five penalty points added to his score.

BIDDING, PLAY AND SCORING

Players, who each start with scores of 12, can bid from one to six, or pass. A bid of six can be overcalled by a bid of Redbeard, which is an all-or-nothing bid and cannot

You will need: 52 cards; scorecard

Card ranking: Standard, Aces high

Players: Three to seven

Ideal for: 14+

be overcalled. The successful bidder becomes the soloist and leads to the first trick. Other players must follow suit, or otherwise play any card. The highest card of the suit led takes the trick, the winner of each trick leading to the next.

A successful bidder of Redbeard sheds as many points as the bid, or, if unsuccessful, goes five up. The other players shed one point per trick. If they take no tricks at all, they go five up, unless they take the option the soloist must give them to drop out after the fourth trick. If they do so, no penalties are incurred, but if they play on, they must take at least one of the final two tricks.

CONCLUSION

The player who is the first to reach zero wins. If he fails to announce this by saying 'Knock for going out' and another player subsequently makes the announcement, he goes five up.

BOURRÉ

This game owes its present popularity in the American South to its successful revival as a Cajun game in Louisiana. It probably descends from a French three-card game, which, in turn came from the Spanish game Burro, meaning donkey.

You will need: 52-card deck; no Jokers; gambling chips/counters
Card ranking: Standard, Aces high
Players: Two to eight, but five and over is optimal
Ideal for: 14+

OBJECT

To win as many of the five tricks as possible. A player who wins three tricks scoops the pool.

THE DEAL AND PLAY

Each player puts the same number of chips into the pot, and is then dealt five cards singly face down. The dealer's last card is dealt face up to indicate trumps. The player to the dealer's left now decides whether to pass or play. This is announced in turn around the table. Players who have decided to play undertake to win at least one trick. They state how many cards – if any – they want to discard, the dealer dealing the replacements from the stock.

The player to the dealer's left leads. Tricks are played for as in Whist, with players having to follow suit, discarding or trumping if they cannot do so. Any player holding the Ace, King or Queen of trumps is obliged to play it as soon as possible.

SCORING AND CONCLUSION

Holding cards that will ensure winning three tricks is termed a 'cinch' and guarantees winning the pot. A player who does not take any tricks is *bourréd* and must pay into the pot the same number of chips as is already there. If two players win two tricks each – this is a split pot – the hand is tied and the pot is carried forward to the next deal.

JULEP

Originally from Spain, this game is firmly established throughout South America. The name literally means 'a sweet drink'.

You will need: 40 card-deck (Tens, Nines and Eights removed from a standard pack); gambling chips/counters for juleps
Card ranking: Ace, Three, King, Queen, Jack, Seven, Six, Five, Four, Two
Players: Three to seven, five to six being ideal
Ideal for: 14+

OBJECT

To take at least two tricks to avoid having to pay sweeteners, *juleps*, as forfeits of chips to other players or into the pot.

THE DEAL

Each player is dealt five cards, the dealer turning up the topmost undealt card to establish trumps. The remaining cards form a stock.

PLAY AND SCORING

Each player can choose to pass, in which case he throws in his hand, or bid to play. This means taking at least two tricks. Players must follow suit or trump. Only if they can do neither can they discard. The highest card of the suit led, or the highest trump, takes the trick. Players who bid to play can discard as many cards as they like, drawing replacements from the stock. If only one player bids, any one player who passes may offer to 'defend the pack' by drawing six new cards from the stock and discarding one of them. The player to the dealer's right leads.

Any player who fails to take a minimum of two tricks has to pay an agreed forfeit, the *julep*, into the pot. If only one player succeeds, he wins the pot plus a *julep* from the other players. If two players win two tricks, they split the pot and *juleps*.

CONCLUSION

If the pack was defended unsuccessfully and lost, the lone bidder wins the pot, but no *julep*. If the defender wins, he gets the pot and a *julep* from the lone player.

FIVE-CARD LOO

This is a typical example of a plain-trick game in which players who think they will be unable to take a single trick or reach a minimum quota of tricks can drop out of the hand before play begins. There are five- and three-card versions, the latter being covered later. The J♣ is known as Pam. It always belongs to the trump suit and beats every other card in the pack, including the Ace of trumps. As well as Loo, other games of this kind include Rams in France and Blesang in Switzerland.

OBJECT

The object is to win at least one trick, each trick earning the player taking it a fifth of the pot.

THE DEAL

Players cut to see who deals first, the player with the lowest card winning – Aces are low for this purpose. The dealer puts five chips into the pot and deals five cards to each player in packets of three and two. The remaining cards are stacked face down to form the stock, the topmost being turned face up to indicate trumps.

FLUSH

A Flush is five cards of the same suit – a plain suit or trumps – or four of a suit plus Pam. The highest Flush is four of a suit plus Pam, followed by a Flush in trumps and then by a plain-suit Flush containing the highest top card. Whoever holds the best Flush 'looes the board', taking all five tricks by default and so winning the game.

SCORING

All the players have the opportunity to stay in or to drop out. Any player who stays in wins a share of the pot in proportion to the number of tricks he takes, but a player failing to win a single trick is deemed to be 'looed' and has to double what is already in the pot.

You will need:	52 cards; no Jokers; gambling chips/counters
Card ranking:	J♣ highest, then standard, Aces high
Players:	Three to eight
Ideal for:	14+

BIDDING, PLAY AND CONCLUSION

Each player in turn announces whether to pass or to play. All the active players then have the right to discard as many cards as they choose in exchange for replacements from the stock. The player to the dealer's left leads. The others must follow suit, if they can, or otherwise play a trump. Only if they can do neither are they permitted to discard. The highest card of the suit led or the highest trump, if any trumps are played, wins the trick.

If the Ace of trumps is led, its leader may say 'Pam, be civil', in which case anyone holding Pam may not play it if there are any other trumps in his hand. Each trick a player takes wins a fifth of the pot, but anyone failing to take a trick must pay a forfeit into it. The winner of each trick leads to the next and must lead a trump if possible.

Below: The J♣ in Five-Card Loo is known as Pam, and beats every other card in the pack, including the Ace of trumps. In this case, if Clubs were trumps, the player holding Pam would beat the A♣.

Left: A Flush is five cards of either a plain suit or trumps, or four of a suit and the J♣ (Pam). The best Flush is four of a suit plus Pam, then a Flush of trumps, then a plain-suit Flush with the highest top card. The player with the best Flush (if any), wins all five possible tricks without play.

NORRLANDSKNACK

The name of this game from the far north of Sweden means 'North Country Knock'. It is related to Ramina, which is played in Finland.

You will need:	52-card deck; gambling chips/counters
Card ranking:	Standard, Aces high
Players:	Three to five
Ideal for:	14+

OBJECT
To lose tricks rather than to win them. The winner is the first player to reach zero points.

THE DEAL
The dealer deals three cards to each player, turns up the next card to establish trumps, and then deals the final two cards. Each player can either knock, so undertaking to take at least one trick, or, on the first deal, say 'I lurk'. This means he won't be penalized for failing to win a trick. Subsequently, the choice is to knock or pass. In the opening deal, a draw follows the initial knock. Every player, except the dealer, who has to take the turned-up trump, can discard and exchange as many cards as he likes. After that, players choose whether to drop out or play.

PLAY, SCORING AND CONCLUSION
Each player puts a chip into the pot and is given a score of 10 points, which goes down a point for every trick a player takes. The player to the left of the dealer leads, playing the Ace of trumps if he holds it. Otherwise, the lead can be any card. In the opening hand, if a knocker fails to take any tricks, he is 'loafed'. This means either adding five to his score, or raising it to 10 if that would make the score more. In subsequent hands, the same penalty applies to all players. They must also put a chip into the pot. The player who reaches zero first, takes the pot.

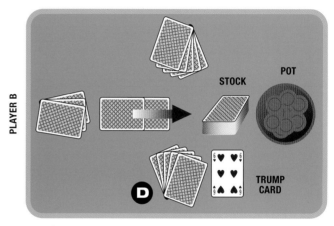

Above: After the deal and knock, every player, except the dealer, who has to take the turned-up trump card, can discard and exchange as many cards as he likes. Here, Player B exchanged two cards.

FEMKORT

The name of this Swedish game translates as Five Cards. It is unusual, as it does not matter how many tricks are won until the last trick is played, and any player may call for 'better cards' during the course of play. There are no trumps.

You will need:	52-card deck; no Jokers; gambling chips/counters
Card ranking:	Standard, Aces high
Players:	Two to ten
Ideal for:	14+

OBJECT
The object is to take the final trick and so win the pot.

THE DEAL
Each player puts an equal number of chips into the pot; this is agreed prior to the start of the game. They are then dealt five cards each in packets of two and three.

PLAY AND CONCLUSION
Each player plays to a trick by laying a card face up on the table. The card is left like that for the remainder of the game, so that all the players can see who has played what. The player to the left of the dealer leads first, play following suit if possible. The highest card of the led suit takes the trick, the winner leading to the next.

If a player calls for 'better cards' and no other player objects to the call, the hand is void and a new deal follows. Otherwise, play continues with the cards as held. The game is won by whoever takes the final trick.

THREE-CARD LOO

This is the older version of Loo, which can trace its origins back to the 17th century. It was a notorious gambling game in the 19th century, when, unless stakes were deliberately limited, fortunes were quickly lost on the turn of a few cards. The rules, conventions and card etiquette are broadly the same as in Five-Card Loo, but there are some important differences. Initially, the dealer puts three chips into the pot – this is termed a 'single'. If the pot contains chips left over from a previous hand, it is a 'double'.

OBJECT

To win at least one trick. A player who fails to win a trick is said to be 'looed' and, as a penalty, must add three chips to the pool.

> **You will need:** 52 cards; no Jokers; gambling chips/counters
> **Card ranking:** J♣ highest, then standard
> **Players:** Up to 17, but five to seven is optimal
> **Ideal for:** 14+

THE DEAL

Everyone starts with an equal number of chips. Each player receives three cards, which are dealt singly, while a spare hand, called Miss, is also dealt. The remaining cards are stacked face down, and the top one is turned up to indicate trumps.

Right: In Three-Card Loo, the first to lead must play the Ace of trumps (here, Spades) if he holds it. If the Ace is the turned-up trump, he must, if possible, lay the King of trumps instead.

PASSING AND EXCHANGING

Each player decides whether to play, in which case the undertaking is to take at least one trick, or to throw in the hand. Any player offering to play is entitled to ask if he can exchange the hand he has been dealt for Miss, but only the first player to request this can actually do so. He does this without looking at Miss (sight unseen) and afterwards cannot drop out or exchange back again.

If every player passes, the dealer scoops the pool, as does the exchanging player if everyone else passes. If only one player plays before the dealer without exchanging, the dealer must either play for his hand – exchanging or not – or elect to 'defend Miss'. In this case, he must still play, but cannot win or lose.

PLAY, SCORING AND CONCLUSION

The leading player must lead the Ace of trumps if he holds it, or, if the Ace is the turned-up trump, the King of trumps, if he has it. Otherwise, he must still lead a trump if he holds more than one in hand. The other players must follow suit and play a higher card if they can. If not, they must trump. Only a player holding no cards of the suit led and no trumps can discard. The highest card of the suit led or the highest trump wins the trick. The winner leads to the next trick, which he must lead with a trump, if possible.

Each trick earns the player who took it a third of the pool. A player who is 'looed', i.e. one who takes no tricks at all, pays three chips into the pot (or an amount agreed in advance before play starts), which is then taken forward as a double. Otherwise, a player who is looed must put in whatever the pool contained at the start of the deal.

Above: Although Three-Card Loo had a bad reputation for being a vicious gambling game, it was also played in the 19th century as a mild domestic pastime, and appeared frequently in the novels of Jane Austen.

TOMATO

This Spanish equivalent of the game Loo is extremely popular in its homeland.

OBJECT

The first player deciding to play after the cards have been dealt must take two tricks, while the others must take at least one trick each to avoid being 'tomatoed'. Each trick taken wins a third of the pot.

THE DEAL

The dealer puts three chips into the pot, after which each player is dealt three cards. Before looking at his hand, the dealer must say 'pass' or 'play'. If the latter, the next card is turned up to establish trumps, after which the dealer discards a card (sight unseen) and picks up the upturned one. This commits him to taking two tricks, and only then does the dealer look at his hand. If the dealer passes, the first to say 'play' goes through the same procedure, though only one trick has to be taken. If all pass,

You will need: 40-card deck (Eights, Nines and Tens having been removed from a standard pack); gambling chips/counters

Card ranking: Ace, Three, King, Queen, Jack, Seven, Six, Five, Four and Two

Players: Three to ten

Ideal for: 14+

the hands are scrapped and the pot is carried forward. The other possibility is for a player to 'defend the pack', which he does by drawing a new hand from the stock. If he takes a trick, the pot is carried forward to the next hand.

PLAY, SCORING AND CONCLUSION

The first active player to the right of the dealer leads. Players must follow suit and beat the card if posssible or, if unable to follow, must trump or overtrump. They may pass only if unable to do either. Each trick taken wins a third of the pot, while a player who wins no tricks is 'tomatoed' and has to double it.

ZWIKKEN

This is the Dutch version of an old Austrian game, Zwicken, once widely played throughout the old Hapsburg Empire until it was banned. Players can decide whether to play for the entire pot or just for part of it, or to pass. Anyone holding a *Zwikk*, three of a kind, automatically wins the game.

OBJECT

To win by either getting the highest *Zwikk*, or taking two tricks, or winning a trick that is worth more card points than those of the other two players added together.

THE DEAL

Players each put a chip into the pot and are dealt three cards – first one, then two – from a 20-card pack. The next card is turned up to set trumps.

PLAY, SCORING AND CONCLUSION

The player offering to play for the highest amount becomes the shooter, the person who undertakes to win by either of the three ways detailed under Object. Before play,

You will need: 20-card deck (Nines and under removed from a standard pack); no Jokers; gambling chips/counters

Card ranking: Ace, King, Queen, Jack, Ten

Players: Three

Ideal for: 14+

a player holding the Ten of trumps may exchange it for the turned-up card. Any player holding a *Zwikk* declares it, and wins the pool. If there are two *Zwikks*, the higher-ranking one wins. If no one has a *Zwikk*, the player to the dealer's left leads. Players must follow suit if possible, otherwise trump, or overtrump. The highest card of the suit led, or the highest trump, wins the trick.

An Ace is worth four points, a King three, a Queen two and a Jack one. A successful shooter wins the stake he played for, but, if not, the same amount must be added to the pot, probably because of the high stakes involved.

Left: One of the aims in Zwikken is to secure three of a kind, the highest being three Aces.

TOEPEN

This noisy cheating game is very popular in Dutch cafés and bars, as the loser has to pay a forfeit, which is usually a round of drinks.

> **You will need:** 52-card deck with Twos to Sixes removed
> **Card ranking:** Ten (highest), Nine, Eight, Seven, Ace, King, Queen and Jack (lowest)
> **Players:** Three to eight
> **Ideal for:** 10+

OBJECT

To lose as few lives as possible, starting with 10, and to take the last trick. The winner of that trick becomes the next dealer.

THE DEAL

From the 32-card deck, four cards are dealt two at a time. Any player with a hand consisting of an Ace and the three court cards may exchange it for a new one, but this opens up the possibility of a challenge from another player, who can insist on turning up the discarded hand.

Left: A player in Toepen with three Tens in his hand must whistle or sing, while one with four Tens must stand up.

If the discarded hand contains cards other than the ones specified, the discarder loses a life for cheating. If not, the challenger loses one. A player with three Tens must whistle, or sing, or, if holding four, stand up. For a player holding three or four Jacks, both conventions are optional.

PLAY AND CONCLUSION

The player to the dealer's left leads and the winner of the final trick deals the next hand; each other player losing a life. Play then follows convention, but a player may knock the table to raise the stakes by an extra life at any stage. Once a player has knocked, he may not do so again until someone else has done so. The others can stay in at the risk of losing a further life for each subsequent knock, or fold.

The game ends when a player loses 10 lives and has to pay an agreed forfeit.

AGURK

This Danish game is popular throughout the Baltic region – *agurk* is Danish for cucumber. Suits have no significance; what counts is the face value of each card. The twist comes in the last trick, when the player taking the trick is penalized.

> **You will need:** 52 cards; no Jokers; gambling chips/counters
> **Card ranking:** Ace is 14, King 13, Queen 12, Jack 11 and the other cards as marked
> **Players:** Three to seven
> **Ideal for:** 10+

OBJECT

To end up with the lowest number of penalty points.

THE DEAL

Players pay the same stake into the pot and are each dealt six cards.

PLAY

The player to the dealer's left leads. Each player after that can play a card with a rank that is at least as high as the highest card previously played, or play his lowest-ranking card. Whoever plays the highest card or, if the cards are of equal value, whoever is the last to play, leads to the next trick.

SCORING AND CONCLUSION

The player taking the final trick is penalized according to its face value (the sum of the cards that make up the trick). Once a player has accumulated 30 penalty points, he is 'cucumbered' and drops out of play. The player can elect to come in again, but, if so, starts with the same number of penalty points as the player with the next highest total. This can be done only once. The pot goes to the player with the lowest total of penalty points when only two players are left in the game.

TRUC

There are several versions of this Spanish game, the one played in Catalonia being the most popular. It is also played with slight variations in the south of France. Played with a Spanish pack, the cards in each suit run from Ace to Seven and Ten to Twelve – the Ten is the Valet, the Eleven is the Horse and the Twelve the King. Suits are Coins, Cups, Swords and Batons. The dealer and the player to the dealer's left are the captains of their respective partnerships, which sit opposite each other at the table.

OBJECT

In each deal, the aim is to win two tricks, or, the first if both sides win one. The first partnership to reach 12 points wins.

BETTING AND SIGNALLING

The hand, and the bets associated with it, is won by the partnership taking two out of the three possible tricks. If there is a tie, the non-dealing partnership wins. While a hand is in progress, players are allowed to talk freely and even signal to their partners. Winking, for instance, means that the player holds a Three, pouting means a Two, and showing the tip of the tongue means an Ace.

THE DEAL

The deal passes to the right after every hand. Three cards are dealt to each player singly. Provided that neither partnership has yet scored 11 points from previous hands, the non-dealing one may propose a one-card deal, in which there is no raising of the stakes. The partnership's captain requests this by tapping on the pack instead of cutting it after shuffling. The dealer can accept or reject the proposal.

Below: Played with a 40-card Spanish pack, the cards used in Truc in each suit run from Ace to Seven and Ten to Twelve, with the Ten called *Sota* (Valet), the Eleven *Cavall* (Horse) and the Twelve *Rei* (King).

You will need: Spanish 40-card pack

Card ranking: Three (highest), Two, Ace, King, Horse, Valet, Seven, Six, Five and Four (lowest)

Players: Four, in partnerships of two

Ideal for: 14+

PLAY

The player to the dealer's right leads. The highest card takes the trick, unless both teams play two or more cards of equal value. In this case, the trick is drawn and goes untaken. The winner of a trick leads to the next.

SCORING AND CONCLUSION

Each hand is initially worth a point, but any player can double this to two by calling '*truc*' either before or after playing a card. The captain of the opposing partnership decides whether to accept the call, or concede. The alternative is for either player in that partnership to call '*retruc*', so raising the stakes by a further point.

When a partnership reaches 11 points – the game is 12 points – the players must decide whether or not they want to play the next hand. If they play, the hand is automatically worth three points and no raising is allowed. If not, the opposing partnership scores a point.

TREIKORT

Treikort is a three-player game that was at one time widely played in Iceland, where it originated. It is closely related to Alkort, another Icelandic card game.

OBJECT

To win as many tricks as possible and take the title of Pope. This means winning 13 tricks over three games.

THE DEAL AND PLAY

Each player is dealt nine cards, three at a time. The player to the dealer's left leads to the first trick. Whichever player plays the highest card takes the trick and leads to the next. Any card may be led at any time with the exception of a Seven. A player cannot lead a Seven until he has taken a trick. The first player to take five tricks scores a point.

You will need: 27 cards: Aces, K♦, Q♣, Jacks, red Nines, Eights, Sevens, Sixes, 4♣, 2♠ and 2♥

Card ranking: Sevens win if led, otherwise they lose, followed by Q♣, 2♠, K♦, 2♥, 4♣, 8♠, 9♥ and 9♦. Aces, Jacks, Sixes and the remaining Eights are worthless

Players: Three

Ideal for: 10+

BECOMING POPE

A player who wins 13 tricks over three games takes the title of Pope. This gives him the right to get one of the two other players to give up his highest card and to take a Seven from the third player – if that player has one in his hand – in exchange for any cards he elects to discard. If the first player has no Seven, the Pope must do without.

The title of Pope is lost as soon as its holder fails to take 13 tricks in any further three consecutive games.

Left: The Sevens in Treikort are unusual in that they cannot be beaten if led but otherwise are worthless.

CONCLUSION

The highest cumulative trick taker at an agreed point wins the game.

PUT

This English version of Truc traces its origins back to the 16th century. Its name derives from the call 'put', made when a player is about to play a card.

OBJECT

To be the first player to score five points.

THE DEAL AND PLAY

Both players contribute the same stake before they cut for the deal, which subsequently alternates. Each player receives three cards, which are dealt to them singly.

The non-dealer leads, the higher ranking of the two cards played winning the trick. If both cards are of equal rank, the trick is tied and the cards discarded.

You will need: 52 cards; no Jokers

Card ranking: Three (highest), Two, Ace, King, Queen, Jack and Ten down to Four (lowest)

Players: Two

Ideal for: 10+

SCORING AND CONCLUSION

A player winning two tricks or one trick to two ties scores a point. If the score is one trick each and the third is tied – this is termed 'trick and tie' – the hand is a draw, as it is if all three tricks are tied. The first player to score five points wins the game. A player can call 'put' while playing a card, in which case the opposing player may either resign and concede the point or play on, in which case the winner of the trick automatically scores five points and so wins the game. If the call of 'put' is made and the result is a tie, no one scores any points.

Left: In Put, any card may be played to a trick, which is taken by the higher-ranking of the two. If both are equal, the trick is tied and discarded.

ALUETTE

Otherwise known as Le Jeu de Vache (The Cow Game), Aluette is played along the French Atlantic coast, where its likely cradle was Nantes. It has many unusual features, including the way cards are ranked and the signalling system employed to indicate which cards individual players hold.

OBJECT

To ensure that just one partner takes more tricks than any other single player.

THE DEAL

Each player is dealt nine cards three at a time, the rest being stacked face down on the table.

RANKING AND SIGNALLING

The card rankings in Aluette are complex. Eight individual cards rank the highest. The first four are termed *Luettes* and consist of the 3♦ (*Monsieur*), the 3♥ (*Madame*), the 2♦ (The One-eyed Man) and the 2♥ (The Cow). Players signal that they are holding these cards by looking up, placing a hand on the heart, closing one eye and pouting respectively. *Doubles* consist of the 9♥ (Big Nine), the 9♦ (Little Nine), the 2♣ (Two of Oak) and the 2♠ (Two of Script). The signals are lifting a thumb, raising a little finger, raising an index finger and pretending to write.

These cards are followed in order by Aces, Kings, Queens, Jacks and Nines down to Threes. Suits do not feature in the game. This means that all Aces are equal in value and will beat Kings, which beat Queens and so on.

PLAY

The player to the left of the dealer leads, after which any card can be played since there is no compulsion to follow suit. The highest card takes the trick and the winner leads to the next. If a trick is tied, it is discarded.

MORDIENNE

This is not compulsory, but is a commonly played extra. If a player is confident that he will not only win the most tricks, but also take them in unbroken succession, he

You will need: 48-card Spanish-style pack, or conventional pack with the four Tens removed

Card ranking: See under 'Ranking and Signalling' below

Players: Four, in partnerships of two

Ideal for: 14+

Above: 19th-century playing cards from the Aluette deck. Aluette is also called Le Jeu de Vache, from the picture of a cow depicted on the Two of Cups.

signals this by biting his lip. If his partner nods back, the bidder says '*Mordienne*' and the contract is made. A successful bid wins its bidder two game points, but, if it fails, they are awarded to the opposing partnership.

SCORING AND CONCLUSION

The player who takes the most tricks individually scores a game point for his partnership. In a tie, the partnership to reach that number of tricks first scores a game point. The first side to score five game points wins the game.

Left: The highest-ranked cards in Aluette are *Luettes* and consist of the 3♦, 3♥, 2♦ and 2♥. These are followed by the *Doubles*, the 9♥, 9♦ and the 2♣ and 2♠.

3 | HEARTS GAMES

WHAT MAKES GAMES OF THIS FAMILY UNIQUE IS THAT THE BASIC AIM IS TO NOT WIN TRICKS, OR AT LEAST TO NOT WIN THOSE THAT CONTAIN CARDS CARRYING A PENALTY. THE SKILL LIES IN KNOWING WHEN TO PLAY YOUR HIGH CARDS AND WIN SAFE TRICKS, LEAVING THE BOGUS CARDS FOR YOUR OPPONENTS TO TAKE. PENALTY CARDS ARE USUALLY HEARTS PLUS THE Q♠, ALTHOUGH IN JACKS AND POLIGNAC, JACKS ARE THE CARDS TO AVOID.

It takes a particular type of card sense to successfully play Hearts and other games in this fascinating family. Cards such as Twos and Threes are as valuable as Aces and Kings in many of these games, and the middle ranks such as Sevens and Eights can be quite dangerous. Most of these games seem straightforward enough on the surface, and all of them are fun to play, but many have an added sting that can sometimes take an unwary player by surprise.

Generally, the best strategy is to aim to take no tricks at all, or at least avoid winning tricks that contain penalty cards. However, this is not necessarily always the case. In some Hearts games, it can pay a player to try to take every trick because if he is successful, his score is reduced rather than increased.

In the Italian game Coteccio ('reverse' in Italian), for instance, the aim is either to avoid taking the greatest number of card penalty points or to win all five tricks. In the latter case, the successful player wins outright. Hearts, the classic trick-avoidance game, has an interesting possible twist. If a player wins all the scoring cards, termed 'hitting the moon', his penalties are reduced by 26 points, or all the other players' scores increase by the same amount.

Above: In Hearts, capturing all the scoring cards, plus the Q♠, is known as 'hitting the moon', and reduces a player's penalties by 26.

HEARTS

First recorded in the USA in the 1880s, Hearts is an extremely popular game with literally dozens of possible variations. Thanks to its success as a computer game, the four-handed version may reasonably be regarded as standard. There are no partnerships as such, although sometimes it pays for two players to collaborate informally. There are no trumps.

OBJECT

To avoid taking any tricks containing penalty cards (the entire Hearts suit and the Q♠) or to capture all 14 of them (termed 'hitting the moon').

You will need: 52-card deck; no Jokers	
Card ranking: Standard, Aces high	
Players: Three to eight, but four most commonly	
Ideal for: 10+	

THE DEAL

Each of the players receives 13 cards dealt singly.

PASSING OF CARDS

After the first deal, each player passes three cards face down to the player to the left and gets the same number from the player to the right. Each player must place the cards to be passed – there is no restriction on what these can be – face down on the table, ready to be picked up by the receiving player. Only then may players pick up the cards that have been passed to them.

The process is repeated on the second and third deals, the difference being that, on the second deal, the cards are passed to the right and received from the left. On the third deal, the players seated opposite each other exchange them. The cycle is repeated until the game is over.

PLAY

Any player holding the 2♣ must lead it to the first trick. If possible, players must follow suit, otherwise playing any card. The person playing the highest card of the led suit takes the trick and leads to the next.

It is against the rules to lead a Heart until one has been discarded – this is 'breaking Hearts' – unless a player holds nothing but Hearts or the only alternative is to lead the Q♠. Nor can any penalty card be played to the first trick unless there is no alternative. Normally, all non-penalty cards won in tricks are discarded on to a waste pile, and penalty cards are turned face up on the table and laid in front of the players who won them. This allows players to work out which penalty cards are still to be played.

SCORING

Every Heart is worth one penalty point, while the Q♠ scores 13 points. If a player manages to 'hit the moon', he can either deduct 26 points from his total, or elect to have all the other players' scores increased by 26 points.

CONCLUSION

The game continues until one player reaches or exceeds a score of 100 penalty points at the end of a hand. The player with the lowest score is the winner.

Left: A typical trick in Hearts. Unable to follow suit, Player C gleefully discards the Q♠. Player D also cannot follow suit, so discards the A♥. Player B unexpectedly finds he has 14 penalty points counting against him.

Below: The cards to avoid in Hearts games are usually Hearts and the Q♠.

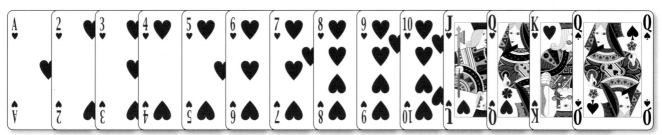

JACKS

Sometimes called Knaves, this penalty-trick game is best described as a cross between Hearts and Polignac. In this game, tricks with Jacks in them score minus points, while tricks without Jacks win plus points.

You will need: 52 cards; no Jokers	
Card ranking: Standard, Aces high	
Players: Three, easily adaptable for more	
Ideal for: 10+	

OBJECT

To take as many tricks as possible without Jacks in them.

THE DEAL AND PLAY

Each player gets 17 cards, the remaining card being turned up to establish trumps. The player to the dealer's left leads, the others following suit if possible. A revoke – that is, not following suit nor playing a trump when able to do so – costs the player concerned three plus points. The trick goes to the player of the highest trump, or the highest card of the led suit.

SCORING

At the end of a hand, each player scores one plus point for every trick he has taken. If, however, he has any Jacks in his tricks, he scores minus points – one for the J♠, two for the J♣, three for the J♦ and four for the J♥.

Left: In Jacks, there is a penalty for each Jack taken in tricks, so the aim is to avoid winning tricks with Jacks in them.

CONCLUSION

The first player to score 20 plus points wins.

POLIGNAC

The French version of Jacks, Polignac dates back to the early 19th century. Its German equivalent is Slobberhannes (Slippery Hans).

Deck: 32 cards for four players, Twos to Sixes removed; 28 cards for five or six players, Twos to Sevens removed	
Card ranking: Standard, Aces high	
Players: Four to six	
Ideal for: 10+	

OBJECT

To avoid taking any tricks with Jacks in them – especially the J♣ (the Polignac).

THE DEAL AND PLAY

The cards are dealt evenly in batches of two or three. The player to the dealer's left leads, the others following suit if they can, otherwise playing any card. The highest card of the led suit takes the trick.

Left: In Polignac, the aim is to avoid taking tricks containing Jacks. The J♣, known as the Polignac, incurs two penalty points, while other Jacks, such as the J♦ here, incur just one penalty point.

SCORING

After each hand, each player scores penalty points for any Jacks taken. If a player takes Polignac, the score is two penalty points. The other Jacks score a point each.

If a player decides to take all the tricks – which is known as 'general' – this must be declared before play. If successful, the other players are penalized five points each. If not, the 'general' gets the penalty and the Jacks are scored as usual.

CONCLUSION

The player with the fewest points after an agreed number of hands wins. Alternatively, the first person to score ten points is the loser.

BARBU

In this complex and skilful game, players take it in turns to be dealer and declarer, each playing seven possible contracts once. This means 28 hands must be played in all to make up a game.

You will need: 52-card deck; no Jokers; scorecard

Card ranking: Ace down to Two

Players: Four

Ideal for: 14+

OBJECT

To make one's contract, or prevent other players from making theirs.

THE DEAL AND CONTRACTS

The dealer deals 13 cards to each player, then declares which of the seven contracts (see box) is to be played. It takes some experience to decide when to declare each contract. It is best to play No Tricks close to the last hand, when playing it with a weak hand is unlikely to prove a disaster. Trumps is best left to last, so that the declarer can be sure of having a hand with four trumps in it.

Doubling and Redoubling

After a contract has been declared, each player in turn may double all or some of the other players, or elect not to do so at all. It is what amounts to a side-bet between two players in which one of them is confident that he will outscore the other, though in the two positive contracts, players are only allowed to double the declarer.

The declarer can only double players who have doubled him, though, over each sequence of seven deals, each player has to double the dealer at least twice. A player who is doubled can redouble the player who doubled him. Saying 'Maximum' means that the player making the announcement is doing that and at the same time doubling any players who have not already doubled him.

PLAY AND SCORING

The declarer starts play. Players must not only follow suit but also play a higher card than the preceding one if possible. If unable to follow suit, any card can be played in a negative contract, or trumps in a positive contract. The highest card played takes the trick, its winner leading to the next. At the end of each hand, all players record the points they have taken in plus or minus columns.

Following this, the results of any doubling are calculated pair by pair, doubles having been recorded on the scorecard as they were made. By convention, the declarer's doubles are ringed to make it easier to check that each

NEGATIVE CONTRACTS

The five contracts (all in No Trumps) are as follows:

- No Tricks – each trick is worth minus two points.
- No Hearts – each Heart scores minus two with the exception of the Ace, which scores minus six. The declarer cannot lead a Heart unless there is nothing else but Hearts in his hand.
- No Queens – each of the four Queens scores minus six points and the hand ends when the last one has been taken.
- No King – the K♥ scores minus 20.
- No Last Two – taking the last trick of the hand scores minus 20, while the penultimate trick is worth minus 10.

POSITIVE CONTRACTS

The two contracts are as follows:

- Trumps – the declarer selects a trump suit.
- Dominoes – the declarer announces a starting rank – e.g. Dominoes from Eights – and plays a card accordingly. The next player must play either a card of the same rank from a different suit or a card of the same suit and adjacent rank to the one that has already been played. These cards are placed face up in a pattern on the table. So, if the card that is led is the 8♠, the next player places a 7♠ or 9♠ to the appropriate side of it or an Eight of a different suit above or below it. A player without such a card has to pass. The first player to lay down all of his cards scores plus 40, the second, plus 20, and the third plus 5. The final player scores minus five.

player has made the two doubles required by the rules. If neither of the two players doubled the other, there is no side-bet. If only one of a pair doubled the other, the difference between their scores is calculated and then added to the score of the player who did better and subtracted from the score of the one who did worse. If one player doubled and the other redoubled, the procedure is the same, but the difference is doubled before being credited to the one and subtracted from the other.

CONCLUSION

Play continues until every trick has been taken. The highest cumulative score at an agreed point wins.

TËTKA

Also known as Tyotka, this game hails from Russia and is widely played throughout eastern Europe. The word *tëtka*, which means 'auntie' in Russian, refers to the Queen of the 'bum suit' in each hand. Both the card and the suit are best avoided or penalty points are incurred. It is virtually impossible to escape all of them, particularly as the game progresses.

OBJECT

To play your hand tactically so that you win only tricks that contain no 'bum cards'. The lowest score (which is the lowest number of penalty points) wins.

THE DEAL

Each player takes it in turn to deal. The first is chosen at random by cutting the pack; and the player with the highest card wins. Four players are dealt 13 cards each singly, the last card being turned up before the dealer adds it to his hand. This becomes the so-called 'bum card'; its suit is the 'bum suit' for that particular deal, and its rank is the 'bum rank'. Play proceeds to the left and a game is any agreed multiple of four deals.

PLAY AND SCORING

The player to the left of the dealer leads, and the other players follow suit if possible. Otherwise, any card may be played. There are no trumps involved. The player of the highest card of the suit that was initially led takes the trick and then leads to the next.

Each penalty incurred scores one point. Penalties are given for the following: for taking a Queen; for taking the Queen of the bum suit (*tëtka*); for taking the bum card in a trick; for winning the 'bumth trick' (i.e. the first if the bum card is an Ace, the second if it is a Two, and so on); for taking the last trick; and for winning the most tricks.

You will need: 52-card deck; scorecard

Card ranking: Standard

Players: Four

Ideal for: 10+

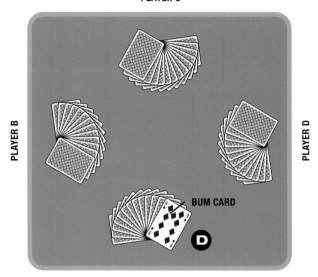

PLAYER C

PLAYER B

PLAYER D

BUM CARD

D

PLAYER A

Above: The last card, turned up by the dealer, becomes the 'bum card', meaning that its suit is the 'bum suit' for that particular deal and its rank the 'bum rank'. Here, then, Diamonds are the bum suit and Nine is the bum rank.

Tactically, it is well worth remembering that several different penalties may be incurred during the course of a single deal. This is a common feature of many so-called compendium games in the Hearts family, of which Tëtka is a classic example. Each of the four Queens, for instance, is worth one penalty point. If more than one Queen is played in a trick, the penalties soon start to mount up. Equally, if a King is the bum card, for example, and a player leads a King at trick 13 (the bumth trick), he would incur two penalty points.

CONCLUSION

Play continues until every trick has been taken. The lowest cumulative score at an agreed point wins the game, a game being any agreed multiple of four deals.

Left: Taking a Queen of any suit incurs a penalty. If a player takes a Queen of the 'bum suit' (*tëtka*), he incurs an extra penalty point.

SCHIEBERAMSCH

This is a trick-avoidance game, the name of which comes from the German word *Schieben* (shove) and *Ramsch* (rubbish). Its complex scoring is similar to that of Skat. Here, however, the undesirable cards (*Skat*) are 'shoved' round from player to player. Jacks are the trump suit.

You will need: 32-card deck (Sixes down to Twos having been removed from a standard pack); scorecard

Card ranking: J♣ is the highest trump, J♠, J♥ and J♦, then Ace to Seven

Players: Three

Ideal for: 14+

OBJECT

To avoid winning the most card points in tricks. However, before play begins, each player has the chance to bid 'grand hand', whereby he undertakes to win at least 61 points in tricks and without picking up the *Skat*.

THE DEAL

Each player is dealt 10 cards as follows: one batch of three (then two extra cards are placed face down on the table to form the *Skat)*, then batches of four and three.

DISCARDING AND CALLING

The player to the dealer's left may pick up the *Skat*, add one or both cards to his hand, and discard an equal number of cards face down in its place to form a new one. Each player in turn may repeat the process. A player with sufficient confidence in his hand can pass the *Skat* on unseen, in which case the loser's eventual score is doubled.

If a player calls 'grand hand', he becomes the soloist, playing against the other two players in partnership. In this case, the *Skat* is not used, but is turned up and added to the soloist's won tricks at the end of play. Either opponent may call '*Kontra*' to double the contract and the soloist can respond with '*Rekontra*', redoubling it.

PLAY

The player to the dealer's left plays the first card. The others follow suit if possible. The highest card of the suit led or the highest Jack wins the trick. The winner of each trick starts the next round. If a non-trump suit is led, a player cannot follow suit by playing its Jack but may trump with another Jack if unable to follow. The player who wins the last trick must take the *Skat*.

SCORING

Each Jack is worth two points. Aces score 11 points, Tens are worth 10, Kings four and Queens three. Nines, Eights and Sevens score zero. The number of points scored by each player is divided by 10, and fractions are rounded down. If all take tricks, the player with the most card points scores that number as a penalty score, increased by as many doubles that apply, then rounded down to the nearest 10. For example, if two players doubled by not taking the *Skat*, and the loser took 64 card points, he scores 4 x 64 = 256 ÷ 10 = 25 (ignoring the remainder). If one player takes no tricks, the player with the most card points scores double (before rounding down). In the event of a tie, both players count the same penalty. If one player takes all the tricks, his penalty score is then reduced by 120.

Grand hand is scored with the 'base value' set at 24 points and multiplied by a 'multiplier' calculated as follows: each Jack is worth a point; two are added for game; and one point for either side getting 90 or more card points (a *Schneider*) or taking all the tricks (a *Schwarz*).

PLAYER C

Above: The layout of the cards after the deal, with two cards for the *Skat*.

CONCLUSION

The player with the cumulative lowest score over an agreed number of hands wins the game.

BASSADEWITZ

Originating in Germany, this uncomplicated game is thought to be a precursor to Ramsch, itself the original version of Schieberamsch. It is still played in parts of German-speaking Europe.

OBJECT

To take as few as possible of the 120 card points available in each hand, and win the pool.

THE DEAL

The dealer puts 12 chips into the pool (or all four players contribute three) and deals eight cards to each player.

PLAY

The player to the dealer's left leads to the first trick, the other players following suit if they can. Otherwise, they play any card. The highest ranked card or highest card of the led suit takes the trick. The winner of each trick leads to the next. There are no trumps.

SCORING AND CONCLUSION

Cards rank and score as follows: each Jack is worth two points, Aces score 11 points, Tens are worth 10, Kings four and Queens three. Nines, Eights and Sevens score zero.

PLAYER C

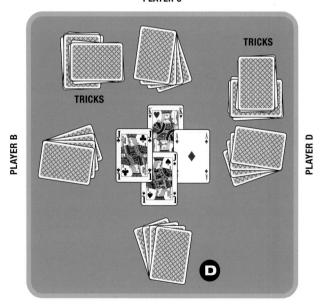

PLAYER A

Above: Player C, having just won a second trick, leads the K♥. Player D tops it with the A♦, Player A tops it again with the J♠, but Player B takes the trick with the J♣, the highest-ranked card.

PLAYER C

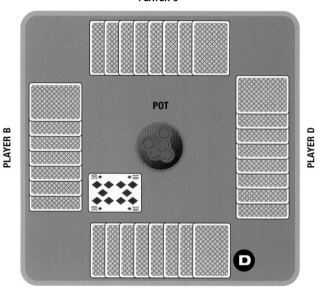

Above: Before dealing eight cards to each player, the dealer has to put 12 chips into the pot (or, upon agreement, each player can put in three).

The player with the lowest number of card points wins five chips from the pool, the second lowest four chips and the third lowest three chips. In the event of a tie, the player who led to the trick wins. A player taking no tricks can beat a player who scores no card points.

If a player takes every trick, he receives four chips from each of the other players. If a player scores 100 card points or more and fails to take all the tricks, he pays four chips to each of his opponents. In both cases, the pool is carried through to the next hand and the same player deals again. This also happens when everyone takes the same number of card points.

VARIANT

In an earlier version of the game, an Ace would count for five penalties instead of 11, and each player would add one per trick to his card-point total. This meant that the maximum score would be 88 when four played.

COTECCIO

The name Coteccio or Cotecchio is applied to various negative point-trick games in Italy. The version that is described here is played in Trieste. It uses the card-points system that is associated with the ancient game of Trappola.

You will need: 40-card deck (Tens, Nines and Eights having been removed from a standard pack); gambling chips/counters

Card ranking: Ace down to Jack, then Seven down to Two

Players: Two to seven

Ideal for: 14+

OBJECT

To avoid taking the most card points in tricks; alternatively to win all the tricks, when the winning player takes the contents of the pot.

THE DEAL AND PLAY

All the players pay agreed equal stakes into the pool and start the game with a notional four 'lives'. Five cards are then dealt to each player in turn, and the remaining spare cards are put to one side.

The player to the dealer's right leads to the first trick. Play proceeds anti-clockwise. The other players must follow suit if possible, or they may play any card. The player who places the highest card of the leading suit wins the trick. The trick is then placed face up in front of the player taking it. The winner of each trick leads on to the next. There are no trumps.

PLAYER C

PLAYER B

POT

SPARE CARDS

D

PLAYER D

TRICKS

PLAYER A

Above: Player A, having taken the first four tricks, can annul the hand, in which case no one loses a 'life', or he can lead the last card. If this wins, he gains a life and the other players lose one. If not, he loses a life and the trick's winner gains one. Here, he gambles on winning the final trick.

SCORING

Aces score six points, the Kings five, the Queens four and the Jacks three. The remaining cards, from the Sevens downwards, score zero. The winner of the last trick scores six. The player with the most points at the end of a hand normally loses a life. If two or more players tie for the most points, they each lose a life. If one player takes all of the first four tricks, he has two options. He can elect to annul the hand, in which case no one loses a life, or he can try to win the fifth trick by leading to it. If his card wins the trick, he gains a life and the other players each lose one. If not, he loses a life and the winner of the trick gains one.

If all four players tie for most of the tricks, which means that they will 'die' at the same time, the entire game is anulled. Players re-start the game with four lives each, and a new pool is added to the old one.

CONCLUSION

In theory, players drop out once they have lost four lives. By agreement, though, a player in this position can opt to 'call the doctor' after paying an extra stake into the pool (provided at least two other players remain alive) and receive as many lives as remain to the player who has the second fewest. Those left alive continue until only one player remains. The last player wins and collects the contents of the pot.

Above: Coteccio is unique among Italian card games for its points system. Of the top four cards, Aces score six points, the Kings score five points, the Queens four points and the Jacks score three.

4 | ACE-TEN GAMES

MANY OF EUROPE'S BEST-KNOWN CARD GAMES ARE TERMED ACE-TEN GAMES, THAT IS, ONES IN WHICH ACES COUNT FOR 11 POINTS, TENS SCORE 10, KINGS FOUR, QUEENS THREE AND JACKS TWO. THE OTHER CARDS ARE USUALLY VALUELESS, AS ARE TRICKS. IT IS SCORING CARD POINTS THAT COUNTS. GAMES ARE USUALLY WON BY TAKING AT LEAST 61 CARD POINTS IN TRICKS, AND PLAYERS ARE ALMOST ALWAYS PENALIZED FOR TAKING FEWER THAN 31 POINTS.

The first Ace-Ten game in card-playing history is Brusquembile, recorded as being played in France as early as 1718. The most celebrated of all is Skat, Germany's national card game. There are many others, each with unique characteristics. In games such as Schafkopf, for instance, some of the Queens and Jacks are permanent trumps whereas in Klaverjas, which originated in the Netherlands, Jacks and Nines, rather than Aces and Tens, are the highest trumps. Players holding the King and Queen of the same suit, Four of a Kind, or sequences of three or more cards in a suit score bonuses. In southern European countries, most notably in Italy and Spain, local packs do not include a Ten. This has not stopped games like Briscola and Madrasso, the latter being a favourite in Venice and the surrounding area, from becoming widely popular. Another card, which is usually the Three, but sometimes the Seven, takes the Ten's place.

All these games are played with stripped-down packs, containing 40, 36, 32, 24 or 20 cards. Reducing the size of the pack has several advantages. It obviously speeds up the game, and has led to the invention of new games ideally suited to three players.

Having fewer cards also introduces variety into trick play and trick-taking. Some tricks are worthless, while others may contain enough high-scoring cards to win the game outright after only a few tricks have been played. Some of these games are extremely complicated to play but are worth the effort.

Above: Skat, which was invented in 1810 in Germany, is now the country's national card game and one of the most celebrated of all Ace-Ten games.

SCHAFKOPF

Widely played in southern Germany, notably in Bavaria where it was invented in 1811, this three- or four-player game exists in many forms. It is played with a 32-card German-suited pack, but here French suits have been substituted.

OBJECT

The aim of the game is to win at least 61 card points of the 120 available. A bonus is awarded for taking 90 or more (*Schneider*), or winning all eight tricks (*Schwarz*).

THE DEAL AND PLAY

Each player is dealt eight cards four at a time. Each in turn says 'Pass' or 'Play'. If all pass, the deal is annulled. If one or more bids, they declare their contract (see box). The player to the left of the dealer leads to the first trick. Players must follow suit if possible, otherwise they may play any card. The highest card of the led suit wins the trick, or the highest trump if played. The winner of each trick leads to the next. Whoever holds the called Ace (see below) must play it when its suit is led, or must lead with it the first time he leads from its suit, unless he holds four or more other cards of the same suit.

CONTRACTS AND BIDDING

After the deal, players either pass or compete for bidding. From lowest to highest, the bidding contracts are:

- Call-Ace – Hearts and *Wenzels* are trumps. The bidder 'calls the Ace' by naming the Ace of a suit other than Hearts (which must be a suit in which he holds a card other than the Q, J and A) and the player holding it becomes the bidder's partner (which is only revealed by play).

- *Wenz* – Jacks are trumps, ranking in their normal order.

- *Suit Solo* – the bidder can nominate a trump suit, which, headed by all the *Wenzels*, forms a series of 14 trumps. The bidder cannot hold any trumps other than *Wenzels*.

- *Solo-Tout* – a bid to take all eight tricks.

- *Sie* – a bid to take eight tricks, using all the *Wenzels*.

- *Kontra* – an opponent may double a contract by saying 'Kontra' at any time up to the playing of the opening trick's second card. The soloist, or soloist's partner, can in turn redouble. In both cases, the side concerned must score at least 61 in order to beat the contract.

You will need: 32-card deck (Sixes and below having been removed from a standard pack); scorecard

Card ranking: Queens and Jacks (*Wenzels*) are the highest trumps, ranked Q♣, Q♠, Q♥, Q♦, J♣, J♠, J♥, J♦. Other trumps and non-trumps: Ace (highest), Ten, King, Nine, Eight and Seven

Players: Three or four, with ad hoc partners from deal to deal

Ideal for: 14+

Left: If a player bids Call-Ace, and asks for the A♦, the holder of this hand will become his partner for the deal, assuming that no other player bids higher. The bidder's hand must contain a Diamond, other than a Q, J or A.

SCORING AND CONCLUSION

Aces are worth 11 points, Tens score 10, Kings four, Queens three and Jacks two. 'Runners' are the top three trumps held in one hand, or by one partnership, together with any more trumps held in downwards succession. They score 10 points each, and this is increased if there is any doubling.

In Call-Ace, the losing players pay 10 points to each of their opponents, or 20 points if they are *Schneidered* (their opponents have taken 90 or more), or 30 points if they are *Schwarzed* (their opponents have won all eight tricks).

In *Wenz* and *Suit Solo*, the soloist can win or lose 50 points or get a bonus of 60 points for *Schneider* and a bonus of 70 points for *Schwarz*. Winning or losing *Solo-Tout* is 100 points, *Sie* is 200 points. Play continues until all the tricks have been played. A game is any multiple of four deals.

Left: German-suited double-headed picture cards. Queens and Jacks are permanent trumps, ranking above Aces.

SKAT

Invented in around 1810 in Germany, Skat has spread across the world. Basically it is a three-handed trick-taking game. Each hand begins with an auction, the winner becoming the declarer and playing alone against a partnership of the other two players. The player to the dealer's left is called Forehand, the one to Forehand's left Middlehand, and the player to Middlehand's left Rearhand.

OBJECT

Usually to win at least 61 card points. There are options to take at least 90 points, or to win or lose all 10 tricks.

THE DEAL

Each player receives 10 cards in packets of three, four and three. The last two cards of the deck, the *Skat*, are placed face down on the table. This takes place after the players receive their first three cards and before the second and third packets of four and three cards are dealt to them.

TYPES OF GAME

Which player will be the declarer, playing alone against the other two players in partnership, is determined by an auction. The declarer's aim is usually to win at least 61 card points, although there are the options of aiming to take at least 90, or to win or lose all 10 tricks. It all depends on which type of game the declarer elects to play – Suit, Grand or Null. In a Suit game, the four Jacks are the highest trumps regardless of suit, followed by the remaining seven cards of the chosen suit. In a Grand game, only the Jacks are trumps, while Null is a bid in which there are no trumps, to lose every trick.

The declarer can also elect to play with the *Skat* or without it. No one else may examine the *Skat* until after the last trick has been played, but any card points it may contain count for the declarer.

GAME VALUES

Players bid by announcing the minimum score of the contract they wish to play (and *not* the name of the contract), which they calculate in advance as follows.

In Trump games, what is termed the 'base value' of the suit chosen as trumps is multiplied by additional factors known as 'multipliers'. The base values are nine

You will need: 32-card pack (Sixes and below having been removed from a standard deck); scorecards

Card ranking: Trumps (except in a Grand game, see below): J♣ (highest), J♠, J♥ and J♦, Ace, Ten, King, Queen, Nine, Eight and Seven. Non-trumps: Ace, Ten, King, Queen, Nine, Eight and Seven

Players: Three (or four, with dealer sitting out hand)

Ideal for: 14+

Above: In a Suit game, the four Jacks are the highest trumps, ranking from high to low according to suit ♣, ♠, ♥, ♦. In a Grand game, only the Jacks are trumps, whereas in a Null game there are no trumps at all.

for Diamonds, 10 for Hearts, 11 for Spades and 12 for Clubs. The base value for a Grand – that is, when only the four Jacks are trumps, is 24.

The multipliers are always taken in the following order, all being added together as you go. *Spitze* (Tops) is based on the number of consecutive top trumps (*Matadors*), from the J♣ downwards, held or not held in hand. If a player holds the J♣, he is 'with' as many *Spitze* as there are in hand. The maximum possible holding is 'with 11' in a Suit game and 'with four' at Grand. If the J♣ is not held, that player is playing 'without' as many of the top trumps that rank above the highest trump in hand. If that trump is the J♠, the player concerned is 'without one' and so on up to a possible maximum of 'without 11' in a Suit game or 'without four' at Grand.

A point is then added for game – 'one for game' – by which the player undertakes to win at least 61 card points. Another point can be added if the intention is to reach *Schneider* (90 points or more) and another point for *Schwarz* (winning every trick).

If a player intends to play from hand without taking the *Skat*, he adds another point – 'one for hand'. If this is the case, then he can also increase the game value by adding one or two extra points for declaring he will win *Schneider* or *Schwarz* as well as the points gained for actually winning either. If declaring *Schwarz*, game value can be further increased by a point for playing *Ouvert* – that is, with the hand exposed on the table.

The lowest possible game value is 18, the highest valued Suit game 216 and the highest Grand is 264. Null games, by contrast, have set values, which never vary. These are 23 for Null with *Skat*, 35 for Null hand, 46 for Null *Ouvert* and 59 for Null *Ouvert* from hand.

BIDDING

Middlehand starts by bidding against Forehand, by announcing successive game values, starting with 18, to which the response is 'Yes' until either Middlehand decides not to bid higher or Forehand passes. Jump bids are allowed (jumping from 18 straight to 33, say), but it is illegal to announce anything but a specified game value.

With the first stage of the auction concluded, Rearhand takes over the bidding. The last player not to pass becomes the declarer. If using the *Skat*, the declarer picks it up, discards two cards and announces what the game is to be. If playing from hand, the word 'hand' is added, together with any other declaration, *Schneider*, *Shwarz* or *Ouvert*. In the last instance, the declarer lays his hand face up on the table before leading the trick.

CONCEDING THE GAME

The declarer has the right to concede the game at any time before he plays to the first trick. There are various reasons for this, the commonest one being that, when playing with *Skat* exchange without two or more *Matadors*, the declarer finds one or more higher *Matadors* in the *Skat*. Suppose, for instance, there is a successful bid of 30, its bidder intending to play in Hearts (Hearts 'without' two, game three, x 10 = 30). If the *Skat* includes the J♣ or J♠, this revalues the bid at 20 ('with' or 'without' one, game two, x 10 = 20).

The declarer now has three choices. He can announce Hearts, as he intended, and attempt to win *Schneider* for the extra multiplier that will increase the game value to 30. He can choose a different game – Spades (22), Null (23), Clubs (24) or Grand (48). If none of these options is playable, then the game is conceded without play.

PLAY AND SCORING

The player to the dealer's left (Forehand) leads and the winner of each trick leads to the next. Suit must be followed if possible, but otherwise any card can be played. The highest card of the suit led or the highest trump, if any are played, takes the trick. All the cards won by the partners should be kept together in a single pile. All 10 tricks have to be played – except if the declarer

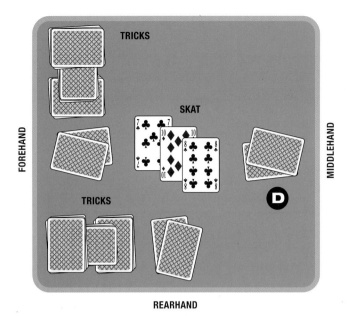

Above: Middlehand here, going for a Null contract, is caught out when the dealer leads the 7♣ and Forehand discards, as he is unable to follow suit. Middlehand's 8♣ wins the trick, meaning that the contract is lost. There is no need to play out the remaining two tricks.

wins a trick and the contract is Null. Once all the tricks have been completed, the *Skat* is turned face up so the game can be valued correctly.

For the declarer to win the game, he must take at least 61 card points – 90 points if the bid was *Schneider*, every trick if the bid was *Schwarz* or no tricks at all if the bid was Null – and the game as revalued after the end of play is worth at least the amount that he bid.

Assuming all these conditions are satisfied, the declarer adds his actual game value to his aggregate score. The *Skat* counts as part of the hand for the purposes of game valuation. This means that it is possible to be 'with' or 'without' 11, even though only 10 cards are actually held in hand.

If the declarer loses a game worth at least the amount bid, its full value is doubled and deducted from his aggregate score. If the value of his game is less than the amount bid, the value to be doubled is defined as the nearest appropriate multiple of the relevant base value that exceeds the bid or equals it, i.e, if his bid was 36, and the game was 30, he loses 40, doubled to 80. If he is *Schneidered*, no extra penalty is applicable.

CONCLUSION

Play continues until all the tricks have been played.

DOPPELKOPF

The north German equivalent of Schafkopf, Doppelkopf is played with a double pack and has an unusual system of 26 trumps. There are a number of somewhat arcane variations.

OBJECT

To take at least 121 card points by capturing valuable cards in tricks.

THE DEAL

Each player is dealt 12 cards each in batches of three. Any player dealt five or more Kings, eight or more Aces and Tens or just one trump, may demand a redeal.

Above: The first hand here has five Kings, while the second has four Tens and four Aces. In each case, the player holding such a hand can demand a redeal.

BIDDING

Players announce '*Gesund*' ('healthy'), meaning that they are happy to play a normal game in which players with the Queens of Clubs ('the grannies') partner each other, or '*Vorbehalt*' ('reservation'), meaning that they want to play some other type of game. In *Vorbehalt*, the first two options are *Hochzeit* (Marriage) or *Armut* (poverty), in both of which the player seeks a partner. A player who, despite holding both grannies, is not confident of playing solo, bids *Hochzeit*. The first player other than the bidder to take a trick becomes the bidder's partner. A player holding three or fewer trumps, which must be placed face down on the table, can bid *Armut*. The partner is the player who picks up these discards and exchanges the same number of cards with the bidder.

The third option is to choose one of eight types of solo. In Trump Solo, the bidder names the trump suit, while in Queen and Jack Solo only Queens or Jacks are trumps. Ace Solo is a No Trumps bid. In Hearts, Spades, Clubs and Diamonds Solo, the respective suits are trumps.

You will need: Two 24-card decks (Eights and below having been removed from two standard packs); scorecards

Card ranking: Trumps: 10♥, 10♥, Queens, Jacks, A♦, A♦, K♦, K♦, 10♦, 10♦, 9♦, 9♦. Clubs and Spades: Ace, Ten, King, Nine. Hearts: Ace, King, Nine

Players: Four, in variable partnerships

Ideal for: 14+

PLAY, SCORING AND CONCLUSION

In a *Gesund* game, the partnership with the Queens of Clubs is dubbed the Re team; in a *Vorbehalt* game, it is the partnership or soloist specifying the game that is Re. The opposing players are know as the *Kontra* team. Announcing '*Re*' or '*Kontra*' doubles the amount of points to be won.

Once a double has been announced, there can be further announcements. 'No 90' is an undertaking to win at least 151 card points, 'No 60' at least 121 and 'No 30' at least 211. *Schwarz* means the players intend to win every trick that is played. If successful, each member of the announcing team wins an extra game point, but if they fail they lose the game. *Re* team players each score a game point for winning at least 121 card points. If the *Kontra* team takes 120 card points, each player wins two game points.

'Catching a fox', won by the team capturing the A♦ (the fox), is worth one game point for each player. *Karlchen Müller* (Charlie Miller), which is winning the last trick with the J♣, scores the same, as does *Doppelkopf*, which is taking a trick where all the cards are Tens and Aces. Note that neither catching a fox or *Karlchen Müller* can be scored in Solo contracts.

Above: Two players holding the Q♣ have the option of partnering with each other, in which case they are dubbed the *Re* team.

Above: Winning a trick containing the A♦ is termed 'catching a fox', and is worth one game point for each player in a partnership. Winning the last trick with the J♣ is termed *Karlchen Müller* (Charlie Miller) and, again, scores a point for both players.

AVINAS

This partnership game hails from Lithuania. It is played in two ways, depending on whether or not Sevens are exposed during the deal.

You will need: 32-card deck (Sixes and below having been removed from a standard pack); scorecard

Card ranking: Q♣ (highest), Sevens, Q♠, Q♥, Q♦, J♣, J♠, J♥, J♦, Aces, Tens, Kings, Nines, Eights

Players: Four, in partnerships of two

Ideal for: 14+

OBJECT

The aim of the declaring side is to take at least 61 of the 120 card points available.

THE DEAL

Each player is dealt eight cards in batches of four, and the dealer exposes everyone's fourth and eighth cards. If no Seven is turned up, the player to the dealer's left chooses a trump suit and states how many trumps he holds without revealing the name of the suit. The other players either pass or quote a higher number of cards held in a suit of their own choosing. The player stating the greatest number of trumps becomes the declarer and leads to the first trick. This is a No Sevens game.

If one of the exposed cards is a Seven then its suit is trumps; if more than one card is a Seven, then the last one dealt becomes the trump suit for that deal. The player who was dealt the Seven of trumps is declarer and will lead to the first trick. This is a Sevens game.

PLAY

In a No Sevens game, the declarer must lead a trump to the first trick. If a Queen or Jack is led and it is unclear what the trump suit is, the player at his left must ask and be answered. The first trick's winner must lead a trump to the second if one is held. All other tricks can be led by any card, and players must follow suit if possible. The declarer may stop play when he realizes he has won or lost.

In a Sevens game, the declarer knocks the table if he aims to take all eight tricks, doubling the value of the game. Opposers can knock to redouble. All the tricks are played, but, if the game is doubled, the declarer loses as soon as his opponents take a trick.

The declarer leads to the first trick. Players must follow suit if possible. The highest card of the suit led, or the highest trump, wins the trick. Normally all eight tricks are played. The declarer wins if he scores more than 61 points, and his opponents are penalized. If not, he is penalized.

Right: As no Sevens feature in the dealt cards, the player to dealer's left chooses a trump suit. The other players can pass or announce a trump suit in turn. He who bids the longest suit sets trumps and becomes the declarer.

SCORING AND CONCLUSION

Aces score 11, Tens 10, Kings four, Queens three and Jacks two. Both games are scored negatively, i.e. marking or cancelling penalties against the losers and winners.

A Sevens game is scored by means of circles called *Avinas* (Rams). If the declarers win, their opponents are penalized by as many *Avinas* as there were Sevens in the deal. If the declarers lose, they are doubly penalized. In subsequent hands, *Avinas* are scored by cancelling those of the opposing side.

A No Sevens game is scored in Pips, written down as a running total. Pips cannot be cancelled. If the declarers win, opponents are penalized one Pip if they score between 31 and 59 card points, two Pips if they take 30 or fewer, and three if they score zero. If the declarers score between 32 and 59, they are penalized two Pips; if they score between two and 31, they are penalized four Pips, and they are penalized six if they score zero.

Play lasts until one side has 12 Pips, while the other has none. If both sides have scored Pips, the game goes to the side with fewer penalty *Avinas*.

PLAYER C

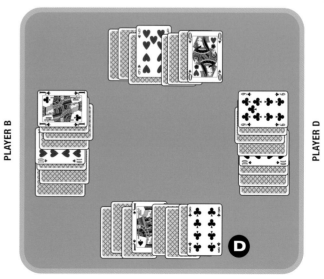

PLAYER B

PLAYER D

PLAYER A

Six-Bid Solo

This is one of three American games – the others are Crazy Solo and Frog – derived from Tappen, which first appeared in southern Germany, western Austria and Switzerland in the early 1800s.

Object

The player who bids the highest value game plays solo against the other two players, competing to win tricks containing valuable point-scoring cards.

Bidding

There are six possible bids, the bidding starting with the two players to the dealer's left. Only after one of them has dropped out is the dealer allowed to participate.

The Deal

Each player is dealt seven cards in packets of four and three, then three are dealt to the table to form a widow, or stock, then each player gets a final four. The widow is left untouched until the end of the game.

Play

Except in Spread *Misère*, when it is the player to the right, the player to the bidder's left always plays the opening lead. Players must follow suit or play a trump card if they can. The highest card of the led suit or highest trump played takes the trick and the winner leads to the next.

Scoring

Aces score 11, Kings four, Queens three, Jacks two and Tens 10. The Eight, Seven and Six are valueless. If the bid is Solo, a successful soloist wins two points from each opponent for every card point taken over 60, but loses two points for every card point taken short of that total if the contract fails. A Heart Solo scores three points, *Misère* 30, Guaranteed Solo 40, Spread *Misère* 60, Call Solo 100 and Call Solo in Hearts 150. Except in *Misère* bids, any card points the widow may contain are added to the soloist's final score.

Conclusion

Play stops once all the tricks have been taken, at which point the player with the highest score wins.

You will need: 36-card deck (Fives and below having been removed from a standard pack); scorecards

Card ranking: Ace (highest) down to Six

Players: Three

Ideal for: 14+

BIDDING

The bids, from lowest to highest, are as follows:

- Solo – an undertaking to win at least 60 card points with any suit other than Hearts as trumps.
- Heart Solo – the same as Solo but with Hearts as trumps.
- Guaranteed Solo – an undertaking to win at least 74 points if playing in Hearts, or 80 if in another suit.
- Call Solo – an undertaking to win 120 points, the soloist having the right to name any card, upon which the holder must surrender it in exchange for a card of the soloist's choice.
- *Misère* – an undertaking to lose every trick (there are no trumps).
- Spread *Misère* – the same as *Misère*, but with the soloist's cards exposed.

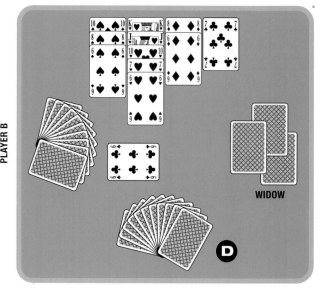

Above: Player C has bid Spread *Misère* (undertaking to lose every trick with his hand exposed). Player B has led the 6♣. Player C will have to play the 7♣ to this, but Player A will have to play higher unless unable to follow suit.

HAFERLTAROCK

This is one of several German games that are obviously derived from Tarock, as Tarot is termed in German-speaking countries, but with the 22 *tarocks* that make up the fifth suit in true Tarot left out. It is definitely not as old as its venerable Italian ancestor, the origins of which date back to the 15th century, but it is a stimulating game to play in its own right.

OBJECT

To win at least 61 of the 120 card points available after naming trumps and playing alone against the other two players.

THE DEAL

Each player gets 11 cards in packets of four, three and four, with three cards being placed face down on the table as a widow (stock) before the final packet is dealt.

BIDDING

As a preliminary, the three players each contribute 100 chips into the pot. Starting with the player to the dealer's left, each player decides whether to pass or say 'Play'.

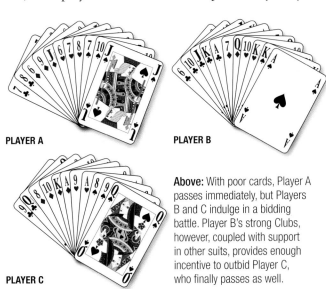

PLAYER A

PLAYER B

PLAYER C

Above: With poor cards, Player A passes immediately, but Players B and C indulge in a bidding battle. Player B's strong Clubs, however, coupled with support in other suits, provides enough incentive to outbid Player C, who finally passes as well.

Player A	Player B	Player C
Pass	Play	Play/Hand
—	And Five	And Ten
—	And Fifteen	And Twenty
—	And Twenty-five	Pass

You will need: 36-card deck (Fives and below having been removed from a standard pack); gambling chips/counters
Card ranking: Ace, Ten, King, Queen, Jack, Nine down to Six
Players: Three
Ideal for: 14+

The latter is a bid to take at least 61 of the 120 card points, playing solo against the other two players and nominating trumps. The next player can take the game off him by bidding 'Hand'. The first bidder can then bid 'Hand' to reassert his bid, or pass. 'And Five', which raises the bid to 66 points, then 'And Ten' and so on, raises the bidding in multiples of five.

This continues until there is a winning bid. The soloist now declares whether the intention is to play a Pick-up or a Hand game. In the former, the soloist picks up the widow and discards three cards before naming trumps. The latter means he will play his dealt hand.

PLAY

The player to the left of the dealer leads to the first trick and play follows convention, with the highest card of the led suit (or the highest trump if any are played) taking the trick. The winner of the trick leads to the next.

SCORING

The scoring cards are Aces, worth 11 points, Tens 10, Kings four, Queens three and Jacks two. The other cards are valueless. Any points in the widow go to the soloist, whether he fulfils his contract or not.

If successful, the soloist wins a basic five chips, plus five chips for every five points in excess of the contract. If the contract fails, the soloist loses five chips for every five points of the shortfall.

If successful in a Pick-up game, the soloist takes the appropriate number of chips from the pot. In a Hand game, the opponents each pay the soloist one chip per point, plus five points for every five points the contract was raised above 61 during the bidding.

CONCLUSION

The game ends when the pot is empty, or by mutual agreement. The winner is the one with the most chips.

EINWERFEN

Einwerfen is a long-established German partnership game and a good one to start with if you are new to Ace-Ten games.

You will need: 32 card-deck (Sixes and below having been removed from a standard pack); scorecard

Card ranking: Ace down to Seven

Players: Four, in partnerships of two

Ideal for: 10+

OBJECT

To win a single game by taking 61+ card points, a double game (90+ points) or a treble for taking every trick.

THE DEAL

Players are dealt eight cards each, the dealer turning up the last one for trumps. The player to the dealer's left leads to the first trick.

SCORING

Aces score 11, Kings four, Queens three, Jacks two, and Tens score 10. The other cards do not score. A partnership scoring 61+ card points wins a single game, a double for 90+, a treble for every trick. If the scores are tied, the value of the next deal is doubled. Any subsequent deal that has the same trumps as the first is doubled in value.

Right: This trick scores four points for the King, 11 for the Ace and three for the Queen, used as a trump: 18 points in all.

Right: This trick scores 10 for the Ten, two for the Jack and 11 for the Ace: 23 points in total.

PLAY AND CONCLUSION

Players must follow suit if they can, play a trump or else play any card. The trick is taken by the highest card of the suit led or the highest trump. The trick's winner leads to the next. Play ends once all tricks have been chased.

YUKON

This Canadian game is a curious blend of elements drawn from Skat and Scotch Whist.

You will need: 52 cards; no Jokers; scorecards

Card ranking: Grand Yukon (J♠), the other Yukons (Jacks), Tens, Aces, Kings, Queens and then Nine to Two

Players: Four, in partnerships of two

Ideal for: 10+

OBJECT

To become the first side to score 250 card points.

THE DEAL

The players receive four cards each. The rest of the pack is placed face down to form the stock, from which players draw the top card after each trick to replenish their hands.

PLAY

The player to the dealer's left leads to the first trick. Players must follow suit if possible or otherwise trump. The Yukons (Jacks) are permanent trumps and they all rank higher than the other cards.

The J♠, the Grand Yukon, takes any trick in which it is played, as does the first played of two or more Yukons (i.e. if two Yukons are played to the same trick, the first one laid wins). Otherwise the highest card of the suit led wins.

Above: The Jacks are the highest-scoring trumps in Yukon.

SCORING AND CONCLUSION

The highest-scoring card is the J♠, worth 15 points, followed by the other Jacks, which score 10, as do Tens. Aces score five, Kings three and Queens two.

The game ends when a partnership scores 250 points. If the stock is used up, play continues until players run out of cards, when the side with the most points wins.

SCOTCH WHIST

In this straightforward partnership point-trick game, players cut the deck to determine partners – the two high cuts play the two low cuts.

OBJECT

To score points by winning tricks, especially those including the top five trumps.

THE DEAL

The person with the lowest cut deals a hand of nine cards to each player. The last card is turned up and its suit is trumps. It belongs to the dealer, but it stays face-up on the table until the dealer plays to the first trick.

PLAY

The player to the dealer's left leads to the first trick. Players must follow suit if they can, or trump or discard. The highest card of the suit led wins. If a trump is played, the highest trump wins. The winner of the trick sets it aside and leads the next trick. Each trick taken after a team 'makes book' (wins six tricks) counts for one point.

You will need: 36-card deck, Fives and below having been removed; no Jokers; scorecard

Card ranking: Standard, Aces high

Players: Four

Ideal for: 10+

SCORING AND CONCLUSION

The Jack of trumps scores 11 card points, followed by the Ace, worth four, King three, Queen two and Ten scores 10. No other cards count. Players score the point value of any top trumps that they may take in tricks, plus an extra point per card for each card they end up with in excess of the number they were dealt. The first partnership to score 41 points wins the game.

Left: Also known as Catch-the-Ten, this interesting game has a venerable history. In his biography of Samuel Johnson, author James Boswell (pictured) referred to Scotch Whist as Catch-Honours.

REUNION

This 18th-century game from the Rhineland consists of three deals – one by each player.

OBJECT

To win the most card points and to avoid ending up with a score of less than 100, as this carries penalties.

THE DEAL

The player who cuts the lowest deals 10 cards in packets of three, four and three, turning up the second of the final two cards for trumps. The dealer discards two cards – not a Bower or an Ace – face down. Any card points they may be worth go to the dealer at the end of the game.

PLAY

The turn-up is left in place until the second trick has been played. The player to the dealer's left leads. Players must follow suit, if possible, or otherwise trump if possible.

You will need: 32 cards, Sixes and below having been removed; gambling chips; scorecard

Card ranking: Jack of trumps (Right Bower), the other Jack of the same colour (Left Bower), Aces, Tens, Kings, Queens, non-trump Jacks, Nines, Eights and Sevens

Players: Three

Ideal for: 10+

SCORING AND CONCLUSION

Each Bower scores 12 card points, Aces 11, Tens 10, Kings four, Queens three and the other Jacks two. The last trick is worth an extra 10 points. If both Bowers are taken in the same trick, the Left Bower's holder immediately pays a chip to the Right Bower's player.

Play continues until the third deal has been completed. Any player with a score of between 100 and 150 pays the winner a chip. If the score is under 100, the penalty is two chips and, if under 50, three.

MADRASSO

Across between Tressette and Briscola, Madrasso is the most popular card game in Venice and its environs. It is usually played with the Venetian patterned 40-card Italian pack, with suits of Swords, Batons, Cups and Coins, equivalent to ♠, ♣, ♥, ♦.

OBJECT

A game consists of at least 10 *Battutes* (deals) and the winning partnership is the first to reach the target score of at least 777 points.

THE DEAL

For the first hand, the dealer is chosen at random; in subsequent hands, the deal passes to the right. Each player is dealt 10 cards, starting with packets of three and two. The next card is turned face up on the table to establish trumps. Three cards each are then dealt to the players, the dealer taking only two, followed by a packet of two cards.

The dealer's face-up card stays on the table until it is played to a trick. However, a player holding the Seven of trumps has the option of exchanging it for the turn-up before playing a card to the first trick.

> **You will need:** 40-card deck (Tens to Eights having been removed from a standard pack); scorecard
>
> **Card ranking:** Ace, Three, King, Queen, Jack and Seven to Two
>
> **Players:** Four, in fixed partnerships
>
> **Ideal for:** 14+

SCORING

At the end of each deal, each side calculates its score, totalling the point value of the cards it has taken in tricks. The scoring cards are Aces, which are worth 11 points, Threes 10, Kings four, Queens three and Jacks two. In the event of a revoke (that is, if a player fails to follow suit when holding a card of that suit), play stops and the revoking partnership is penalized 130 points. The winners of the last trick receive a 10-point bonus.

PLAY AND CONCLUSION

The player to the dealer's right leads to the first trick. Players must follow suit if possible, otherwise any card can be played. Each trick is won by the highest trump in it, or, if no trumps are played, by the highest card of the suit led. The winner of each trick leads to the next. Each hand is played until all 10 tricks have been won.

After 10 hands have been played, any player can make a declaration claiming to have reached the 777-point target immediately after taking a trick. Play stops immediately, the claim is checked, the score of the non-scoring partnership being calculated by subtracting the scoring side's total from 1,300. If the claim is upheld, the declaring partnership wins. If it is not upheld, it loses. If neither has reached that total, the game resumes until one does, or one partnership declares that it is out.

Another way of winning is termed *Cappotto*, which means taking all of the 10 tricks in a hand. This is why declarations are not allowed until 10 hands have been played. Even if one partnership has scored 777 points by the eighth or ninth hands, the other could still make *Cappotto* and so steal the game.

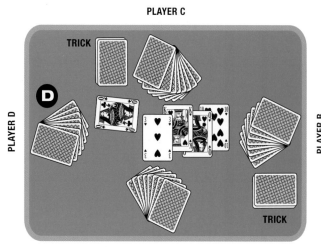

PLAYER C

PLAYER D

PLAYER B

PLAYER A

Above: Players B and C here have both won a trick. The dealer's turn-up card (used to determine trumps), the Q♣, is still exposed on the table. Player B lays the 10♥, which is topped by the Queen, King and Three in succession. Player A wins the trick, as Three is highest.

Right: The scoring cards in Madrasso are Aces (worth 11 points), Threes (10), Kings (four), Queens (three) and Jacks (two).

BRISCOLA

One of Italy's most popular card games, Briscola is most notable for the various facial expressions that are allowed as a way of signalling between partners.

OBJECT

To be the first player or partnership to score a game (at least 61 cards points) or a rubber (three games).

THE DEAL

The player cutting the lowest card is the first to deal – the deal subsequently passes to the right. Each player is dealt three cards face down, the next card being turned face up to set trumps. The remaining cards are placed face down on the table to form the stock.

PLAY

The player to the dealer's right leads to the first trick. Unlike most other card games, there is no obligation to follow suit for as long as any cards remain in the stock. The winner of each trick takes the top card from the stock to replenish his hand, followed by all the other players in turn.

When the stock is exhausted, the next to play draws the turn-up and the game continues until all the cards have been played.

Above: A group of men playing cards in Palermo, Sicily, 2004. Briscola remains one of Italy's most popular card games.

> **You will need:** 52-card deck with Tens to Eights removed; plus a Two removed if three are playing; scorecards
>
> **Card ranking:** Ace highest, then Threes, Kings, Queens, Jacks and Sevens to Twos
>
> **Players:** Two to three playing solo, or four in partnerships
>
> **Ideal for:** 10+

SCORING AND CONCLUSION

Aces score 11 points, Threes score 10 points, Kings four points, Queens three points and Jacks score two. The remaining cards are valueless. A two-way or three-way split of card points at the end of a game is a draw. A rubber is the best of five games, a game equating to at least 61 points.

Play continues in each hand until all the tricks have been won. The player or partnership taking the majority of the 120 card points available wins a game.

> ### SIGNALS
>
> When four people play, certain signals are allowed in Briscola so that partnerships can signal certain trump holdings to each other, when neither opponent is looking. These conventional signs are codified as follows:
>
> - Ace – go tight-lipped.
> - Three – twist the mouth sideways.
> - King – raise eyes upwards.
> - Queen – show the tip of the tongue.
> - Jack – shrug shoulders.

VARIANT

A chief five-player variant of Briscola is Briscola Bastarda. The chief differences are the introduction of a round of bidding and a secret partnership between the winning bidder and another player.

In the bidding, players estimate the number of points they will take in the game. The highest bidder names a specific card to establish the trump suit and who his partner will be. This is the holder of the specified card. The scores of the caller and holder count together. If the total equals or exceeds the bid, the caller wins two points, the holder a point and each opponent is penalized a point. If the bid is lost, each opponent wins a point, the holder is penalized a point and the caller two.

5 | KING-QUEEN GAMES

As the saying goes, marriages are made in heaven. In King-Queen games any player declaring the 'Marriage' of the King and Queen of the same suit in the same hand wins bonuses. Typically, a non-trump Marriage scores 20 points, while a trump (Royal) one scores 40. Such games are exceptionally fascinating because, as every experienced card player knows, their outcome is so unpredictable.

There are several games that share the same basic system of trick-taking and card values, although some introduce an extra element of bidding. Of these intriguing games, the German game Sechsundsechzig (Sixty-Six) – and its Austrian equivalent Schnapsen – is probably one of the best known. It is an exciting game because nearly every card in the deck counts. This means that a player who looks sure to lose can suddenly turn a game on its head and emerge as its winner.

The basic aim is to win points by capturing the most valuable cards and to score bonuses by melding Marriages (matching Kings and Queens). However, there are specific features that make play even more challenging and stimulating. For instance, in many games, players are not allowed to keep scorecards, so they need really clear heads in order to keep track of what is going on as well as good card sense to make the most of the cards.

In Spain and some Latin American countries, Tute is a popular card game. In it, declaring a Marriage is referred to as 'singing' it. A player is only allowed to 'sing' immediately after he has taken a trick. Mariás is the most popular card game in the Czech Republic and Slovakia. Tysiacha, an Eastern European game, is less well known than it should be. Its peculiarity is that bidding must start at 100 points, which means that higher bids can only be fulfilled by declaring King-Queen marriages.

Above: Melding Marriages of the King and Queen of the same suit gains a player bonuses in this group of games.

Sechsundsechzig (Sixty-Six)

This is one of the best card games for two players. Although there is some doubt as to when and where it was invented, Sixty-Six has probably been played at least since the 17th century.

You will need: 52-card deck with Eights and below removed
Card ranking: Ace (highest), Ten, King, Queen, Jack and Nine
Players: Two
Ideal for: 14+

Object

To make Marriages of King and Queens in the same suit or score tricks containing certain cards, and thus to be the first player in each deal to take 66 points.

The Deal

Each player gets six cards, dealt in two packets of three. The next card is turned up to establish trumps and half covered with the rest of the cards (the stock) face down.

Play

Initially, suit need not be followed, the winner of each trick being the higher card of the suit led or the higher trump. Once a trick has been played, both players (starting with whoever won the trick) replenish their hands with a card from the stock.

After the stock has run out, suit must be followed and no more Marriages may be melded. The stock is often closed before this by a player who thinks 66 points can be won with the cards as they stand. Either player may close when it is their turn to lead by flipping over the turn-up and placing it face down on top of the stock.

Trumps and Marriages

A player with the Nine of trumps can exchange it for the turn-up, provided it is still covered by at least two cards and he has taken a trick. If a player is dealt a Marriage or melds one with a card from the stock, he can claim 20 points for a non-trump Marriage and 40 for a trump one, provided that he has taken a trick, is about to lead to a trick, and at least two cards remain in the stock. The declaring player must lead one of the Marriage cards to the trick. If a player declares a Marriage but fails to take any subsequent tricks, its score is cancelled.

Scoring and Conclusion

Players must keep a mental note of their running score. The Ace, Ten, King, Queen, Jack and Nine count for 11, 10, four, three, two and zero points, respectively. After the last trick, or earlier if either player claims to have reached 66 points, the hand is scored. In the first case, the player with the most points wins. In the second, if 66 points have been scored, the declarer scores a game point if the opposing score is 33 points or more, two if under 33, and three if zero. If the claim is incorrect, the other player scores two game points, or three if he has not taken a trick. If a player closes and subsequently fails to score 66 points, the penalties are the same. The first player to take seven game points wins the game.

Play in each hand continues until all tricks have been played or until a player claims to have scored 66 points.

Above: The scoring cards are Aces (worth 11 points), Tens (worth 10), Kings (worth four), Queens (worth three) and Jacks (worth two).

PLAYER B

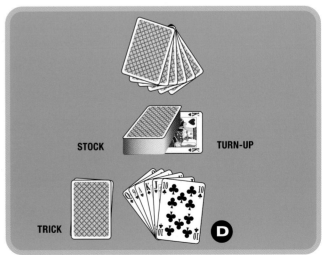

PLAYER A

Above: A player who is holding the Nine of trumps (the 9♥) can exchange it for the turned-up card, provided he has already taken a trick and that the stock contains at least three cards.

BONDTOLVA

This is a traditional Swedish favourite, the name of which translates as 'farmer's dozen'. Roughly speaking, it is the Swedish equivalent of Sixty-Six, but with a few quirks of its own. The simplest version is for two players.

OBJECT

To be the first to get to 12 points by melding Marriages (King and Queen of same suit), winning *Matadors* (Aces and Tens) and taking the last trick.

THE DEAL

The two players are dealt six cards each, three at a time, the other cards being stacked face down to form the stock.

PLAY

The first player to declare a Marriage establishes which suit is trumps. The non-dealer leads. Each trick is taken by the higher card of the suit led, or by the higher trump once trumps have been fixed, but players do not have to follow suit or trump. The winner of each trick draws the top card of the stock, followed by the other player, and leads to the next trick. Once the stock is exhausted no Marriages are allowed; the second to play must follow suit, playing a higher card if possible, or play a trump.

You will need: 52-card deck with Eights and below removed

Card ranking: Ace, Ten, King, Queen, Jack and Nine

Players: Two

Ideal for: 14+

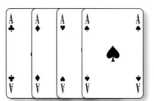 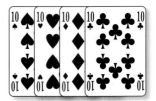

Above: In Bondtolva, Aces and Tens, the top- and second top-ranking trumps, are known as *Matadors*.

SCORING

Aces score four points, Kings three, Queens two and Jacks one. The Nine is valueless. The first Marriage to be declared scores two points; subsequent Marriages score a point. The bonus for winning the last trick is a point, as is the bonus for taking the majority of Aces and Tens. If the scores are equal, the point for the latter goes to the player with the most card points. If the scores are still equal, neither player scores the bonus point. To win the game, a player needs to score exactly 12 points.

CONCLUSION

Play in each hand continues until all tricks have been played or until a player scores 12 points. A player scoring over 12 must deduct the excess from his previous total.

VARIANTS

There are three- and four-player versions of the game, which are played in much the same way with a few minor differences. The four-player version is played in partnerships. Before trumps are established, the player leading the trick can ask if his partner holds a Marriage, or, if holding one card of a Marriage, if the partner can pair it. The next trick must then be started, if possible, from the declared Marriage. Once trumps are fixed, a player can ask the first question again, in which case that suit must be led to win the point, or lead a King or a Queen and ask the partner to wed it.

PLAYER B

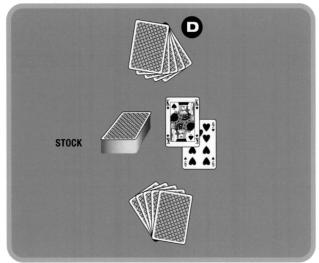

STOCK

PLAYER A

Above: Player A has led the 9♥ to the first trick. Since no Marriages have been melded yet, there are no trumps, so Player B, unable to follow suit, discards the K♠. Player A therefore wins the trick and picks up a card from the stock, followed by Player B.

TUTE

One of the most popular card games in Spain and in Spanish-speaking Latin America, Tute exists in many forms. The two-player version called Tute Corriento is the oldest form of the game and is the one described here.

OBJECT

To be the first to score 101 points by winning tricks, declaring Marriages and taking the last trick.

THE DEAL

The two players deal in turn, six cards to each player. The next card is placed face up on the table to determine the trump suit. The remaining cards are placed face down across it to form the stock.

PLAY

The non-dealer leads to the first trick. Until the stock is exhausted, there is no need to follow suit or trump. The winner of a trick draws the top card of the stock and the loser draws the next. The face-up trump forms the last card of the stock. When the stock runs out, the second to play must follow suit, playing a higher card if he can, or, if possible, trumping.

EXCHANGING AND SINGING

A turned-up Ace, Three or court card (a King, Queen or Jack) can be exchanged for the Seven of trumps. If a Four, Five, Six or Seven, it can be exchanged for the Two of trumps. To signal an exchange, a player places the appropriate card under the turned-up one, and the exchange occurs when that player takes a trick. If the stock runs out before then, the original card is reclaimed.

A player who holds the King and Queen of the same suit can score extra points by declaring ('singing') them, and showing the two cards. This can only be done immediately after winning a trick and before leading to the next. A player having more than one such combination must win another trick before being allowed to declare it. However, if a player holds four Kings or Queens (a *tute*), he can sing them after winning a trick and immediately wins the game. If a player has a Marriage in a trump and a non-trump suit, the trump suit must be declared first. When declaring a Marriage in a non-trump suit, the suit should be named.

You will need: 52-card deck with Tens to Eights removed

Card ranking: Ace, Three, King, Queen, Jack and then Seven to Two

Players: Two

Ideal for: 14+

SCORING

Aces score 11 points, Threes 10, Kings four, Queens three and Jacks two. Ten points are awarded to the player taking the last trick. A non-trump Marriage (King and Queen of same suit) scores 20 points and a trump Marriage (King and Queen of trump suit) scores 40.

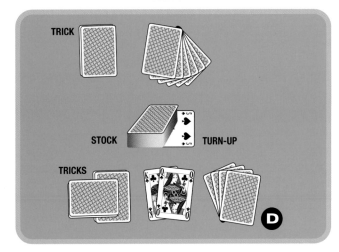

PLAYER B

TRICK

STOCK   TURN-UP

TRICKS

PLAYER A

Above: Player A here, having just won a second trick to Player B's one, sings a Marriage by showing a King and Queen of the same suit. Trumps being Spades, this is a non-trump Marriage, which scores 20 points.

CONCLUSION

Declaring a *Tute* wins the game outright. Otherwise, after the last trick, both players count the points they have won for cards in tricks, singing Marriage and for taking the last trick. If neither has scored 101 points, there is a second deal, the points won in that being added to those taken in the first. If either player thinks that he has scored 101 points, this can be declared and play stops. Such a declaration must be made immediately before leading a trick. If the claim is correct, the declaring player wins; if not, he loses.

TYSIACHA

In Russian-speaking countries, this three-player game is known by the above name. In Poland, it is called Tysiac. Both words mean '1,001' – the target score needed to win the game, and are basically the same game, but with slight variations.

You will need: 24 card-deck (Eights and below having been removed from a standard pack); scorecard

Card ranking: Ace, Ten, King, Queen, Jack and Nine

Players: Three, or four with dealer sitting out the hand

Ideal for: 14+

OBJECT

To be the first to score 1,001 points or more.

THE DEAL

Seven cards are dealt singly to each player. Three cards, termed the *prikup*, are then dealt face down on the table.

BIDDING

Following the deal, players bid to determine who will be the soloist against the other two players. The first bid must be at least 100 points, following which bids go up in fives. Bids over 120 are not allowed unless the player making the bid has a Marriage in hand.

The soloist takes the *Prikup*. He can increase the bid, or, if he decides there is little likelihood of honouring it, he can declare *Rospisat* (that he concedes). In this case, each opposing player scores 60 points. A player declaring *Rospisat* is not penalized on the first two occasions, but on the third, and every third time thereafter, 120 points are deducted from his score.

The soloist passes a card face down to each opponent, so that all three players have eight cards in hand. Any player holding the four Nines can now opt to show them and ask for a new deal.

PLAY

Trumps are established when the first Marriage is declared, although they can be changed by the declaration of a subsequent Marriage. Declaring a Marriage involves showing both cards, announcing their suit and leading either of them to the next trick.

SCORING AND CONCLUSION

An Ace scores 11, Ten 10, King four, Queen three, Jack two and Nine zero card points. A Marriage (King and Queen of same suit) scores 100 points in Hearts, 80 in Diamonds, 60 in Clubs and 40 in Spades. If the soloist scores at least the value of the bid, this is added to his score. If not, the value is subtracted from it. The other

Left: If a player holding this hand is passed a fourth Nine by the soloist, he can call for a new deal.

players score the full value of card points taken in tricks, rounding them up or down to the nearest five, plus the value of any Marriages they may have melded.

Scoring between 880 and 1,000 is against the rules. If this happens, the player is said to be 'on the barrel', a fact indicated by drawing a box on his scorecard. The score is pegged at 880 and the player is given three chances to score 120 points and win the game. In the event of failure, the player 'falls off the barrel' and is penalized 120 points. If either opposing player fails to take any points in tricks three times, he is penalized 120 points on the third occasion. From that point onward, he loses 120 points every third time this occurs. Play continues until all the tricks have been played.

Right: In Tysiacha, a Marriage of the King and Queen of Spades scores 40 points, in Hearts 100 points, in Diamonds 80 points and in Clubs 60 points.

GAIGEL

This game has spread from southern Germany and Switzerland to the USA, where it has been adapted for two players. It is a three- or four-player game, the latter played in partnerships. There is no universally accepted set of rules, and the game is played differently from place to place. The partnership version is described here.

OBJECT

To be the first side to win or exceed 101 points in counters and Marriages, or to detect that the opposing side has done so and failed to claim their win before leading to the next trick.

THE DEAL AND PLAY

After shuffling the two 24-card packs together, each player is dealt five cards, and the next card is turned up to establish trumps. The cards left over form the stock. As long as there are cards left in the stock, there is no necessity to follow suit, but when it is exhausted, players must do so, head the trick if possible (play a higher card than any so far played to the trick), or otherwise trump and overtrump. A trick's winner draws the top card of the stock, the other players then drawing in turn.

You will need: Two 52-card decks, each with Nines, Eights and cards below Seven removed; counters

Card ranking: Ace (highest), Ten, King, Queen, Jack, Seven

Players: Three, or four playing in partnerships. The partnership version is explained here

Ideal for: 14+

When players play to a trick, they are allowed to declare a Marriage (King and Queen of same suit) if they hold one, but no more than one Marriage in the same deal. Such a declaration can be made only if the declaring partnership has already taken a trick, or if the card to be played takes the trick for them. The declaring player shows both cards and then plays one of them. A non-trump Marriage scores 20 points, a trump one 40.

TAKING THE TURN-UP

A player with the Seven of trumps, the *Dix*, can exchange it for the turn-up at any time, provided that the partnership has taken at least one trick and at least three cards remain in the stock.

Alternatively, the player can place the Seven under the turn-up for his partner to pick up if he holds the other Seven. His partner may decide to take the turn-up and pass across the other Seven. If he is not holding the other Seven and one of the opposing partners then plays it, the first player can pick up the turn-up immediately.

SCORING

Aces score 11 points, Tens 10 and the court cards – Kings, Queens and Jacks – score four, three and two points respectively. Sevens are worthless and count for nothing.

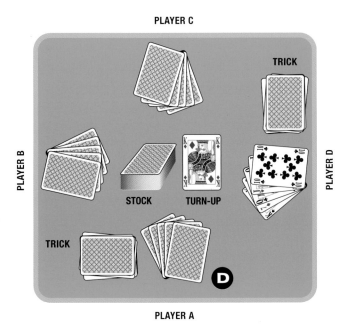

PLAYER C

TRICK

PLAYER B

PLAYER D

STOCK   **TURN-UP**

TRICK

D

PLAYER A

Above: Holding the Seven of trumps (known as the *Dix*), Player D can exchange it for the turn-up at any time, provided the partnership has taken at least one trick and the stock contains at least three cards.

CONCLUSION

Play stops when either side claims to have taken 101 or more points, or when the opposing partnership has done so but neglected to declare it before leading to the next trick. If correct, the claiming partnership wins a single game. If its opponents have not taken a trick, they win a double game or *Gaigel*. If the claim is wrong, the other side wins a *Gaigel*. Claiming a win incorrectly is known as 'overgaigling' and failing to claim a win is 'undergaigling'.

MARIÁS

Closely related to the Hungarian game Ulti, the most popular version of Mariás is for three players, although four can play it. In the three-player game, one player becomes the soloist, playing against the other two in partnership. In its Czech homeland, Mariás is customarily played with a 32-card German-suited pack, but here a reduced standard pack has been substituted.

OBJECT

To win a clear majority of the points available. This is at least 90, but can rise as high as 190 when Marriage declarations are taken into account.

You will need: 52-card deck with Sixes and below removed
Card ranking: Aces, Tens, Kings, Queens, Jacks, Nines, Eights and Sevens
Players: Three, or four with the dealer sitting out the hand
Ideal for: 14+

THE DEAL

The first dealer is chosen at random, after which the deal passes to the left for each subsequent hand. Before the deal, the player to the dealer's right must cut the 32-card pack. The dealer then gives a packet of seven cards face-down to Forehand (the player to the dealer's left) and continues dealing clockwise in packets of five, so that after two rounds of dealing, Forehand has 12 cards and the other two players each have 10. At this stage, Forehand is only allowed to pick up and look at the first seven cards dealt; Forehand's other five cards are left face down on the table until trumps have been chosen. The other players may look at all 10 of their cards.

Right: In Mariás, Aces and Tens are the only scoring cards. Known as 'sharp cards', they are worth 10 points each. Points are also scored for melds and winning the last trick.

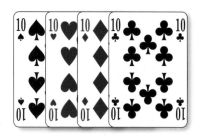

Below: After the deal, Forehand can only look at the first seven cards he has been dealt and choose a trump suit from them should he wish. The strong Diamond suit looks a good bet.

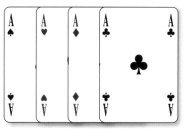

CHOOSING TRUMPS

Forehand proposes a trump suit, bids first and leads to the first trick, the next being Middlehand and the third Rearhand. To choose trumps, Forehand examines the first seven cards in his hand. If he elects to choose the trump suit from them, he turns up the appropriate card. If not, he can 'choose from the people' – that is, by selecting any card from the five remaining ones sight unseen, turning it up as before. He then takes all the cards except for the turn-up and discards two, face down. An Ace or Ten cannot be discarded and if the discards include a trump, Forehand must say so.

CHOOSING THE CONTRACT

Forehand starts by bidding Suit, a game with trumps, that only he can play as soloist. Either opponent can veto this by bidding *Betl* or *Durch*. Both are no-trump bids. In *Betl*, the opposing players win if they can force the soloist into taking a trick. In *Durch*, the soloist loses if his opponents win a trick. There are open options for each bid in which players' cards are placed face up on the table after the first trick has been played. Such bids double the score. In Suit, the soloist has to win more points than the combined scores of the opposing players.

Various bonuses augment scores. For the soloist, Seven is an undertaking to win the last trick with the Seven of trumps; Hundred is one to win 100 points or more without melding more than one Marriage.

Both bids can be combined. A Double Seven is an undertaking to win the last trick with a Seven and the trick before that with another one. The opposing players can make identical announcements by adding 'Against' to the bids.

DOUBLING AND REDOUBLING

To double, either of the opposing players can call 'Flek', the soloist having the option of redoubling by calling 'Re'. The opponents can then double again by saying 'Tutti', which the soloist can redouble by announcing 'Retutti'. How this is done depends on the type of contract.

If *Betl* or *Durch* is to be played, the option to double goes hand in hand with the final determination of the contract. There are three possible responses to its announcement: 'Good', which means that it is accepted as it stands; 'Bad', which means that the player making the call is prepared to play higher; and 'Flek', which doubles the contract's value as explained above. In a Suit contract, the opponents simply answer 'Good' or 'Bad'. As well as starting the doubling processes, players can now announce for which bonuses they intend to play.

PLAY

In Suit contracts, following suit, playing a higher card of the same suit to lead to the trick or playing a trump is obligatory, if possible. In non-trump contracts, the first two conditions apply. In a Suit contract, any player announcing a Marriage (King and Queen of same suit) must play the Queen and announce the appropriate score before playing the King. The cards of a Marriage

Above: An example of 18th-century German playing cards showing the four suits of Acorns, Leaves, Hearts and Bells. In its Czech homeland, Mariás is traditionally played with a 32-card German-suited pack.

are kept separate from the trick and left face up in front of the player scoring them, so that they can be checked afterwards when scores are totalled.

SCORING AND CONCLUSION

Play continues until all tricks have been played. Aces and Tens, known as the 'sharp cards', are the only cards to score and are worth 10 points each. Melding a non-trump Marriage scores 20 points, and melding a trump Marriage scores 40. A further 10 points are awarded for taking the last trick. A successful Suit contract scores a point for game, while *Betl* scores five points and *Durch* scores 10 points.

Unannounced bonuses are worth a point for Quiet Seven and Killed Quiet Seven – that is, when the Seven of trumps is beaten on the last trick – and two for Quiet Hundred. In this, every extra 10 scored over 100 is worth another two points. Announced bonuses – Seven, Seven Against, Killed Seven, Hundred and Hundred Against – score double. All bonus scores are also doubled if the trump suit was Hearts. Revoking costs the offender 20 points – 10 to each of the other players – or the value of the contract plus bonuses, whichever is more. If Forehand bids the basic game and no extras are added or doubles made, it is taken that the opposing players have conceded, and Forehand scores accordingly.

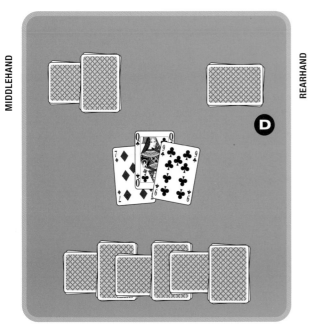

Above: Forehand not only takes the final trick (winning seven to his opponents' combined total of three) but does so with the Seven of trumps (in this case, Diamonds). If he had announced during the bidding the intention of winning the last trick with the Seven of trumps, he would have scored two bonus points. Unannounced, he scores a single extra point.

6 | QUEEN-JACK GAMES

GAMES SUCH AS BEZIQUE AND PINOCHLE STAND THE CONCEPT OF MARRIAGE ON ITS HEAD BY ALLOWING MELDS (SETS OF MATCHING CARDS) BETWEEN THE Q♠ AND THE J♦. THESE ARE KNOWN AS BEZIQUES AND CAN BE EITHER SINGLE OR DOUBLE. THERE ARE ALSO SCORES FOR HOLDING FOUR OF A KIND, OR SAME-SUIT SEQUENCES. IN BEZIQUE, EVEN IF A PLAYER STARTS WITH POOR CARDS, SKILFUL BUILDING OF MELDS MEANS THAT HE MAY WELL END UP A WINNER.

Although originally conceived for only two players, other versions of Bezique for more players developed, while the size of the deck, originally 32 cards, also increased to make games last longer. Two-pack Bezique was all the rage in Paris in the 1840s, while Rubicon Bezique, which is played with four decks totalling 128 cards, originated in London slightly later. Chinese Bezique, which was Sir Winston Churchill's favourite card game, is played with six packs.

Pinochle, the American counterpart of Bezique, remains one of the country's most popular card games. Its basic form is Two-handed Pinochle, although Partnership Pinochle, Partnership Auction Pinochle and Double-Pack Pinochle are all games for four players, two against two as partners. Auction Pinochle is the most popular form of the game for three. In general terms, players score for melds and tricks that contain specified scoring cards. The game can seem over-complex, particularly in the second stage of the game, when players have to take back the cards in the melds they have previously declared, but it more than repays the effort of learning it.

Marjolet is an elegant game for two players that is popular in southwest France. As in other games of this genre, part of the excitement comes from the balancing of the cards that are played to tricks against those that are kept in hand in the hope of making melds. To heighten the tension, some players allow the scoring of only one meld after winning a trick.

Above: Original boxed set of the Royal game of Bezique, which was manufactured by Godall & Son, London (1910).

BEZIQUE

A game called Hoc, played at Louis XIV's court at Versailles, may be the origin of Bezique. The improved two-pack version then became the height of fashion in Paris in the 1840s.

You will need: 64 cards (two standard packs with all cards below Seven removed)

Card ranking: Ace, Ten, King, Queen, Jack, Nine, Eight and Seven

Players: Two

Ideal for: 14+

OBJECT

To be the first to reach 1,000 points over as many deals as necessary, dealing alternately.

THE DEAL

Eight cards are dealt to each player in packets of three, two and three. The next card is turned up to establish trumps and the remaining cards are placed face down to form the stock. If the turn-up is a Seven, the dealer scores 10.

PLAY

The non-dealer leads. The trick is taken by the higher-ranking card of the suit led, or by a trump. At this stage, there is no need to follow suit. If both players play the same card, the leading card takes the trick. The winner of the trick can declare a scoring combination, laying the cards face up. These can still be used to take future tricks and to help to form new combinations, although they cannot be used twice in the same combination. The declaring player draws the top card of the stock followed by the opposing player, and leads to the next trick.

A player with the Seven of trumps may exchange it for the trump turn-up after taking a trick as an alternative to declaring a combination.

SCORING

Brisques (Aces and Tens) taken in tricks score 10 points. Scoring combinations, from highest to lowest, are:

- Double Bezique (two Q♠ and two J♦): 500 points.
- Same-suit sequence of Ace, Ten, King, Queen and Jack of trumps: 250 points.
- Any four Aces: 100 points.
- Any four Kings: 80 points.
- Any four Queens: 60 points.
- Any four Jacks: 40 points.
- Single Bezique (between Q♠ and J♦): 40 points.
- Royal Marriage (between the King and Queen of trumps): 40 points.
- Common Marriage of a non-trump King and Queen: 20 points.

Also, any player may show a Seven of trumps and win 10 points. There are 10 bonus points for winning the last trick.

CONCLUSION

Once the stock is exhausted, suit must be followed and trumps played if this is impossible. The player taking the final trick wins a bonus 10 points. No further declarations are allowed. Play continues until one player has reached or exceeded a total of 1,000 points. If the losing player has scored under 500 points, he is 'rubiconed', and the winner scores a double game.

500 POINTS **250 POINTS** **100 POINTS**

80 POINTS **60 POINTS** **40 POINTS**

40 POINTS **40 POINTS** **20 POINTS**

Above: Scoring combinations in Bezique, assuming Hearts as trumps.

Marjolet

Simpler to play than Bezique, Marjolet allows the Jack of trumps – the Marjolet – to be melded (matched) to the four different Queens. Indeed, a Queen may be melded to the Marjolet and to her matching King at the same time.

Object

To score points by taking Aces and Tens, so-called *Brisques*, in tricks and by declaring melds (sets of matched cards).

The Deal

Both players receive six cards. The next card turned up sets trumps; the remainder of the pack forms the stock.

Play

There is no need to follow suit. The trick is taken by the higher card of the suit led, or by a trump played to a non- trump lead. Both players take a card from the stock. The player who won the trick leads to the next. Before this, the winner can declare any meld. All melds are placed face up in front of the declaring player. His cards can still be used in trick play and to make other melds.

> **You will need:** 52-card deck with Sixes and below removed
>
> **Card ranking:** Ace, Ten, King, Queen, Jack and Nine to Seven
>
> **Players:** Two
>
> **Ideal for:** 14+

Once the stock runs out, both players take their melds into hand. For the last six tricks, suit must be followed and a higher card played, if possible. Otherwise, a trump must be played, again if possible. Melds may still be declared.

Scoring

If the Seven of trumps (the *Dix*) is turned up at the start of play by the dealer, he wins 10 points, while a player holding it can exchange it for the turn-up after taking a trick. The score for the exchange is 10 points. If the player opts not to exchange, the *Dix* still scores 10 when it is played, regardless of whether the trick is won or lost.

Winning the last trick is worth a bonus of 10 points, while, should a player succeed in taking all six tricks, he receives a bonus of 50 points. Each player then sorts through the cards he has won and scores 10 for each *Brisque* he has taken.

MELDS

The winner of a trick can declare any of the following melds:

- Four Aces – 100 points.
- Four Tens – 80 points.
- Four Kings – 60 points.
- Four Queens – 40 points.
- Marriage between the King and Queen of trumps – 40 points.
- Marriage between the King and Queen of a non-trump suit – 20 points.
- Marriage between the Jack of trumps and any trump or non-trump Queen – 20 points.

100 POINTS   80 POINTS   60 POINTS

40 POINTS   40 POINTS   20 POINTS   20 POINTS

Above: Scoring combinations in Marjolet, assuming Hearts as trumps.

Conclusion

Play continues until all tricks have been taken. The winning score can be either 500 or 1,000 points.

    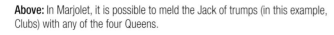

Above: In Marjolet, it is possible to meld the Jack of trumps (in this example, Clubs) with any of the four Queens.

PINOCHLE

Closely related to Bezique, Pinochle started life in the USA as a two-player game, but there are now three- and four-handed versions, plus ones for five or more players. Auction Pinochle, described here, is the most popular three-handed form.

You will need: Two 24-card decks (Eights and below having been removed from two standard packs)

Card ranking: Ace, Ten, King, Queen, Jack and Nine

Players: Three in this version, although can be two to five

Ideal for: 14+

OBJECT

To make as many points as bid from melds (matches) declared from hand after taking the widow. Card points are made in tricks, with extra for winning the last trick.

THE DEAL AND BIDDING

Each player is dealt 15 cards three at a time. Three cards are placed face down to form the widow (stock). The player to the dealer's left bids first. All bids must be multiples of 10 and the opening one must be at least 300 (unless agreed otherwise). The highest bidder takes the widow, discarding three cards face down, announces trumps and declares any melds. If these fulfil his bid, there is no play and he scores the value of his game.

The bidder can also concede if he doubts he can fulfil his bid in play. He loses only his game value, as opposed to twice the game value if he plays and fails.

PLAY

The bidder leads to the first trick. Suit must be followed and, if possible, a player has to 'kill', that is, play a higher card of the same suit. If not, a trump must be played. Otherwise, a player can 'slough' or discard any card. The highest card of the suit led, or the highest trump if any are played, wins the trick. The trick's winner leads to the next.

MELDS

All versions of the game employ the same standard melds:

- Flush (Ace, King, Queen and Jack of trumps) – 150 points.
- Royal Marriage (King and Queen of trumps) – 40 points.
- Plain Marriage (non-trump King and Queen) – 20 points.
- Aces around (four Aces, one of each suit) – 100 points.
- Kings around (four Kings, one of each suit) – 80 points.
- Queens around (four Queens, one of each suit) – 60 points.
- Jacks around (four Jacks, one of each suit) – 40 points.
- Pinochle (Q♠ and J♦) – 40 points.
- *Dix* or *Deece* (Nine of trumps) – 10 points.

SCORING

There are two ways of scoring points, through melding combinations and winning scoring cards in tricks. Aces, Tens and Kings are called counters and are worth 10 points each, while Queens, Jacks and Nines count for nothing. The winner of the last trick scores an extra 10 points.

If the bid is made, the bidder scores the points taken in melds and play. If not, the bidder 'goes out' with the bid being deducted from his score. The other players score the same way, provided that they have captured at least one counter. If not, they score nothing. All scores are doubled when Spades are trumps. Frequently, although not always, Hearts as trumps triple the scores.

150 POINTS **100 POINTS** **80 POINTS**

40 POINTS **40 POINTS** **40 POINTS**

20 POINTS **10 POINTS**

Above: The above are all standard scoring melds or cards, where Hearts are trumps. Other scoring melds can be included by prior agreement.

CONCLUSION

Play continues until all tricks have been taken. The first player to score 1,500 or more points wins.

7 | JACK-NINE GAMES

WHAT DIFFERENTIATES THESE GAMES FROM OTHERS OF THE MARRIAGE FAMILY IS THE PROMOTION OF THE JACK TO THE HIGHEST-RANKING TRUMP, WITH A VALUE OF 20, FOLLOWED BY THE NINE WITH A VALUE OF 14. BELOTE IS THE NATIONAL GAME OF FRANCE, AND KLAVERJAS THE FAVOURITE IN THE NETHERLANDS, WHILE IN SWITZERLAND AND AUSTRIA, JACK-NINE GAMES ARE UNIVERSALLY POPULAR. THE GAMES ARE SO SIMILAR THAT IF YOU MASTER ONE IT IS EASY TO LEARN ANOTHER.

Although authorities on the history of card games agree that the first Jack-Nine games probably originated in the Netherlands, it was undoubtedly the Swiss who honed them until they reached their present sophisticated status. Indeed, these so-called Jass games have become so popular in Switzerland that others which have nothing to do with them have been classified as kinds of Jass, while Swiss cards have come to be known as Jass cards.

A standard Jass pack consists of 36 cards in suits of Bells, Shields, Acorns and Flowers. The French-suit equivalents are Hearts, Diamonds, Clubs and Spades. The name Jass (pronounced 'yass') is thought to originate from Jasper, which was the Dutch name for the knave in the 18th century.

The French version, Belote, became the most popular card game in the country in the mid-20th century. A close relative of Klaberjass and of Klaverjas, the Dutch national card game, it has spawned many variants of its own. Of these, the most interesting is probably Coinche, which now rivals its precursor in the popularity stakes. It has one particularly novel feature. In order to make a declaration during the bidding stage of the game, players have to bang their fists on the table. Schieber Jass, a long-established Swiss game for four players playing in partnerships, also has an unusual feature – an elaborate scoring system, in which, at least traditionally, scores are chalked on a slate painted with two Zs.

Above: A Swiss card deck, also known as Jass cards, which consist of 36 cards in suits of Bells, Shields, Acorns and Flowers.

KLABERJASS

This popular two-hander is known in Britain as Clob, Clobby or Clobiosh, while in the USA it is known as Klob, Kalabriasze or Klabber. It is also sometimes called Bela. In trumps, the Jack and Nine – the *Jass* and the *Menel* or *Mi* – are promoted over the Ace. As well as the two-player version, there are three- and four-player variants.

OBJECT

To reach or exceed a total of 500 points.

THE DEAL

Each player receives six cards three at a time. The next card is turned up to establish a possible trump suit and the remainder placed face down to form the stock. Once trumps have been decided (see below), three more cards are dealt to both. A player holding the Seven of trumps, the *Dix*, can then exchange it for the trump turn-up.

BIDDING

The bidding that follows establishes whether either player accepts the turned-up suit as trumps. The non-dealer can either pass, say 'Take it' or say '*Schmeiss*'.

Left: In trumps (here, assumed as Spades) the Jack (known as the *Jass*) and Nine (known as the *Menel*, or *Mi*), rank above the Ace.

Below: A same-suit sequence of three in Klaberjass is a *Terz* and scores 20 points, but it would score nothing if the other player holds a better sequence. This could either be one of three cards running Queen, King or Ace, or a sequence of four cards or more, known as a *Halbe*, which counts for 50.

You will need: 32-card deck (Sixes and below having been removed from a standard pack); scorecards

Card ranking: Ace, Ten, King, Queen, Jack, Nine, Eight, Seven, except in trumps, where the *Jass* (Jack of trumps) ranks highest, followed by the *Menel* (Nine of trumps)

Players: Two (though three to four versions exist)

Ideal for: 14+

Schmeiss is an offer to become the Maker with the turned suit as trumps and has to be agreed by the dealer. Otherwise, the deal is annulled. If the non-dealer passes, the dealer has the same choices.

PLAY AND SCORING

Before the trick is led, either player holding a sequence of three or more cards must announce the fact. A *Terz*, a sequence of three cards, is worth 20 points, while a *Halbe*, a sequence of four or more, counts for 50. It is only the player with the best sequence who can score. Any *Halbe* beats a *Terz*, a *Terz* with a higher top card beats one with a lower top card, and a *Terz* in trumps is better than one in a plain suit. To determine who has the best sequence, the non-dealer announces 'Twenty' or 'Fifty' on leading to the first trick. The dealer replies 'Good' if he cannot match the number, or 'Not Good' if he can beat it. The questions 'How many cards?', 'How high?' and 'In trumps?' can also be asked.

A *Belle*, the King and Queen of trumps, is worth 20 points. Unlike the preceding melds, or matches, it is not announced until one of its cards is played to a trick. A *60-Terz* is the term applied to describe a *Terz* of the King, Queen and Jack of trumps. It is worth 60 points.

Winning the last trick scores 10 extra points. The *Jass* is worth 20 points, Nines 14, Aces 11, Tens 10, Kings four, Queens three and the other Jacks two.

CONCLUSION

At the end of the hand, both players declare their totals. If the Maker has scored higher, both players score the points they made. If not, his opponent scores the total made by both players. If equal, the Maker scores nothing and the opposing player scores what he took. The first to score 500 or more points in melds and card points wins.

BELOTE

Although it came to France only in about 1914, Belote is now the country's most popular card game. Two, three or four players can play it, but the four-player partnership version described here is the one most often played.

You will need: 52-card deck wtih Sixes and below removed

Card ranking: Trumps: Jack, Nine, Ace, Ten, King, Queen, Eight and Seven. Plain suits: Ace, Ten, King, Queen, Jack and Nine to Seven

Players: Two to three, or four in partnerships of two, as here

Ideal for: 14+

OBJECT

To score as many points as possible through taking tricks and making melds (matches).

THE DEAL

Five cards are dealt to each player three and two at a time. The next card is turned face up. The player to the dealer's right can now 'take' (that is, choose the suit of the turned-up card as trumps) or pass. If the latter, each player gets the same option. If all pass, each has another chance to 'take', this time, naming a trump suit other than the turn-up. If everyone passes again, there is a new deal but the pack is not shuffled. The player who 'takes' becomes the Taker and picks up the turn-up. The others are dealt three more cards, with the Taker getting two.

PLAY

The player to the dealer's right leads. Players must follow suit, trump, over- or undertrump, or discard any card.

SCORING AND CONCLUSION

The Jack of trumps is worth 20 points, the Nine of trumps 14, Aces 11, Tens 10, Kings four, Queens three and the other Jacks two. The other Nines, Eights and Sevens are valueless. When declaring *Belote* and *Rebelote*, *Belote* is

MELDS

Various types of meld score, namely:

- *Carré* (Four of a Kind – can consist of all four Jacks, Nines, Aces, Tens, Kings or Queens) – four Jacks scores 200 points, four Nines 150 and the others 100 points each.
- *Cent* (a sequence of five or more cards of the same suit) – 50.
- *Cinquante* (a sequence of four cards of the same suit) – 50.
- *Tierce* (a sequence of three cards of the same suit) – 20.
- *Belote* and *Rebelote* (the King and Queen of trumps) – 20.

declared first, followed by *Rebelote* when the Queen is played. Apart from this, only the partnership with the highest declaration can score.

The last trick scores an extra 10 points, the *Dix de Der*, for the partnership winning it. If the taker's partnership wins at least as many points as its opponents, both sides score all the points they have made. If not, they are *dedans* (inside). Their opponents score 162 points, to which they add the value of the taking side's declarations plus their own. If the taker's partnership wins all nine, it scores *Capot* (100 points) not *Dix de Der*.

Play continues until one partnership has scored 1,000 or 1,500 points (as agreed before play starts).

200 POINTS

150 POINTS

100 POINTS

100 POINTS

100 POINTS

100 POINTS

50 POINTS

50 POINTS

20 POINTS

20 POINTS

Left: Standard scoring melds or cards in Belote, assuming Hearts as trumps.

COINCHE

This is a popular version of Belote, with the unique feature that players have to bang the table to signal a declaration. Its name derives from the twist that players can *coincher* (double) and redouble each other's bids.

OBJECT
To score points through taking tricks, holding the King and Queen of trumps, or achieving the highest meld.

THE DEAL
The players are dealt eight cards before bidding starts.

BIDDING
Whether or not there is a trump suit depends on the contract to be played – a suit contract, a no trump contract or an all trump one. In the bidding, the aim is to take more than half the trick points available and to score more points in tricks and melds (matched set of cards) than the other partnership. The convention is to bid a number followed by a contract, the lowest permissible number being 80. Subsequent bids go up in multiples of 10. Bidding ends when the other players all pass, or when an opponent doubles the bid, unless the bidding partnership redoubles. The traditional way of signalling a double is to bang a first on the table – in fact, *coinche* means 'fist' in French.

When declaring *Belote* and *Rebelote*, *Belote* is declared first, followed by *Rebelote,* when the Queen is played. Apart from this, only the partnership with the highest declaration can score. If two declarations appear equal, the second to declare asks 'How high?' and the previous declarer must give a clearer and truthful indication accordingly.

You will need: 52-card deck minus Sixes and below; scorecards

Card ranking: Trumps: Jack, Nine, Ace, Ten, King, Queen, Eight and Seven. Plain suits: Ace, Ten, King, Queen, Jack and Nine to Seven

Players: Four, in partnerships of two

Ideal for: 14+

MELDS

On playing to the first trick, players announce their highest meld – the possible combinations are the same as in Belote, namely:

- *Carré* (Four of a Kind) – four Jacks scores 200 points, four Nines 150, and four Aces, Tens, Kings or Queens 100 points.
- *Cent* (a sequence of five or more cards of the same suit) – 50.
- *Cinquante* (a sequence of four cards of the same suit) – 50.
- *Tierce* (a sequence of three cards of the same suit) – 20.
- *Belote* and *Rebelote* (the King and Queen of trumps) – 20.

PLAY
If the lead is a trump, players must follow suit, playing a higher card if possible. If a plain suit is led, it is not necessary to head the trick (play a higher card). If an opponent is winning with a trump, a higher one must be played, but if it is a partner any card can be discarded.

SCORING AND CONCLUSION
At the end of play, both partnerships calculate how much they have won in trick-points and melds. Aces are worth 200 points, Tens 150, and Kings, Queens, Jacks 100 each. Taking the last trick is worth 10 points, while announcing *Belote* and *Rebelote,* the King and Queen of trumps, scores 20 points, except in a non-trump contract.

If the declaring partnership is successful, both sides score the points that they have made and the declarers add the value of the contract to their total. If not, they score zero, their opponents winning 160 trick points, the value of their melds and the value of the lost contract. All scores are affected by any doubling. Game is 3,000 points.

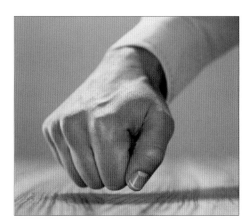

Left: An unusual feature of Coinche is that players have to bang the table to signal a declaration.

Left: When declaring *Belote* and *Rebelote* (the King and Queen of trumps, which here are Clubs), *Belote* is declared first, followed by *Rebelote* when the Queen is played.

BOONAKEN

Closely related to another Dutch game called Pandoeren, this is faster, less complicated and decidedly less serious. In all probability, it gets its name from the Dutch for the three highest trumps – *Boer*, *Nel*, *Aass*, or Jack, Nine, Ace.

OBJECT

To find a loser, who has to pay for a round of drinks.

BIDDING

The player to the left of the dealer bids first. A number bid is an undertaking to win that many points in tricks and *Roem*, which are specific card combinations (see Scoring). A no-trump bid to lose every trick is *Misère* and a bid to take them all is *Zwabber*. *Boonaak* is the same as *Zwabber* but with trumps. *Boonaak* plus a number is a bid to win all the tricks plus that score in *Roem*. Bidding continues until three players pass in succession.

THE DEAL

Six cards each are dealt three at a time, and two cards are placed face up on the table, one after each packet has been dealt. The successful bidder uses these cards to improve his hand by exchanging and discarding. If the bid is a number or a *Boonaak*, he also chooses the trump suit.

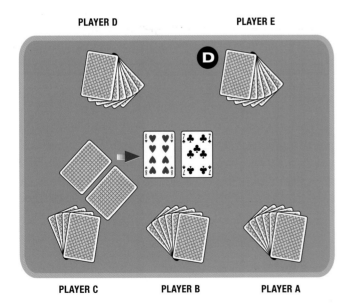

Above: The declarer (Player C), can improve his hand by exchanging up to two cards with the two in the centre. Having bid *Misère*, Player C in this instance discards two high cards and picks up the 8♥ and 7♣.

You will need: 32-card deck (Sixes and below having been removed from a standard pack); scorecard

Card ranking: Trumps: Jack (highest), Nine, Ace, King, Queen, Ten, Eight, Seven. Plain suits: Ace (highest) down to Seven

Players: Five is optimal

Ideal for: 14+

PLAY

The successful bidder leads to the first trick. If the bid is a number bid, he must also announce *Roem* at this stage. The amount announced must be equal to or more than the number bid. If an opposing player has *Roem* in hand worth at least as much as the *Roem* the successful bidder has announced, he announces it as well. If it is worth more than the bidder's, the latter's *Roem* is cancelled and does not count towards winning the contract.

If a trump is led, the other players must follow suit, unless the only one held is the Jack of trumps, when any card can be discarded. When a plain suit is led, that suit must be followed or a trump played. A player is allowed to trump even though suit could have been followed.

SCORING

In the trump suit, Jack scores 20, Nine 14, Ace 11, King three, Queen two, Ten 10, while Eight and Seven score zero. Plain suits (those that are not trumps) score 11 for the Ace, three for the King, two for the Queen, one for the Jack and 10 for the Ten, cards below Ten not scoring. There are no bonus points for taking the last trick.

Roem also scores, provided that the *Roem* held by any opposing players are not higher. A sequence of three cards in a suit scores 20, four 50, five 100 and six 200. Four Jacks are worth 200 points, Aces, Kings and Queens 100 points and the King and Queen of trumps (*Stuk*) 20 points.

CONCLUSION

In a number contract, the declarer wins if trick-points and *Roem* equal or exceed the amount of the bid. Other contracts are scored as might be expected. All scores are entered on a scorecard, a win being marked by a plus and a loss by a minus. A player with two pluses is a winner and can sit out the game. A player with two minuses is the loser.

KLAVERJAS

Extremely popular in its Dutch homeland, Klaverjas is distinguished from other games of this genre because melds (matched sets of cards) are scored as they occur within individual tricks.

OBJECT

To win more than half of the available points in each hand if your partnership has chosen trumps, otherwise to prevent the opposing partnership from scoring these points. Ultimately, the aim is to score as many points as possible over 16 hands.

THE DEAL

From the 32-card deck, each player is dealt eight cards in packets of three, two and three.

CHOOSING TRUMPS

Trumps are determined in either of two ways. Free choice means that the player to the dealer's left can either nominate a trump suit or pass. If he passes, the next player has the same choice. If all four players pass, the player to the dealer's left must decide.

The alternative is to choose trumps at random by turning up the top card of a second deck. The player to the dealer's left either accepts this card as trumps or passes. If he passes, the next player chooses. If everyone passes, a second card is turned up. Its suit automatically becomes trumps.

You will need: 52-card deck wtih Sixes and below removed

Card ranking: Trumps: Jack, Nine, Ace, Ten, King, Queen, Eight, Seven. Plain suits: Ace, Ten, King, Queen, Jack, Nine, Eight and Seven

Players: Four, in partnerships of two

Ideal for: 14+

MELDS

Melds score as follows:

- Three consecutive cards of the same suit – 20 points.
- Four consecutive cards of the same suit – 50 points.
- Four of a Kind (except Jacks) – 100 points.
- Four Jacks – 200 points.
- A Marriage of the King and Queen of trumps (known as *Stuk*) – 20 points.

PLAY

The player to the dealer's left leads to the first trick. The others must follow suit if possible. If no trumps are played, the highest card of the suit led takes the trick. If the trick contains trumps, the highest trump wins. Before leading to the next trick, the winner of the previous one scores the value of any *Roems* (melds).

Signalling between partners is accepted. Discarding a low card of a particular suit, for instance, means the player holds its Ace, while discarding a court card (King, Queen or Jack) is a warning not to lead that suit.

SCORING AND CONCLUSION

In the trump suit, the Jack is worth 20 points, the Nine 14, Ace 11, Ten 10, King four and Queen three. In non-trump suits, Aces score 11 points, Tens 10, Kings four, Queens three and Jacks two. If the partnership choosing trumps wins more than half of the available points, both sides keep the points they have taken. If not, the partnership scores nothing and its opponents take all the points, including bonuses. The winner of the last trick gets a 10-point bonus. Play continues until 1,500 points have been scored.

PLAYER C

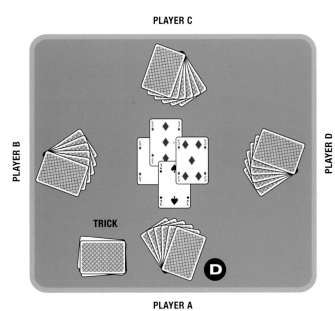

PLAYER B

PLAYER D

TRICK

PLAYER A

Left: Signalling through discards is a feature of Klaverjas. A low discard, such as the 2♠ played here, is used by Player A to show he holds an Ace of that suit (A♠). Discarding a court card is a warning not to lead that card's suit.

HANDJASS

Like its Swiss and western Austrian counterparts, this Jass game revolves around points, which can be scored for three features known as *Stöck*, *Wys* and *Stich* (Marriages, melds and tricks). In its homeland, it is played with a 36-card Jass pack with its suits of Acorns, Shields, Bells and Flowers.

> **You will need:** 52-card deck with Fives and below removed; scorecards
>
> **Card ranking:** Jack of trumps (highest), Nine of trumps, Aces, Kings, Queens, other Jacks, Tens, Nines, Eights, Sevens. Sixes
>
> **Players:** Two to five, although four is optimal
>
> **Ideal for:** 14+

OBJECT

To score at least 21 game points for melds (matched sets of cards) in hand and counting cards captured in tricks.

THE DEAL

Each player gets nine cards in batches of three. If two are playing, two extra hands of nine are dealt. One of these is spare. This means that each player in turn, starting with the one to the dealer's left, has the right to replace the hand he has been dealt with the spare. The other hand is dead and its top card is turned up for trumps.

If three play, the remaining cards are laid down as a spare hand, but the top card is turned for trumps. If four play, there is no spare hand and the dealer's last card is shown to determine trumps. If five play, each deals in turn and then sits out that hand.

Left: The highest-scoring cards in Handjass are the Jack of trumps (known as the *Puur* and worth 20 points) and the Nine of trumps (known as the *Näll* and worth 14 points). Here, Diamonds are trumps.

MELDS

Same-suit sequences are allowed, as are groups. Only the player with the best meld in hand can score for melds. Four Jacks are worth 200 points, four Nines 150 and four of any other numbered card 100. If there are two quartets of cards worth 100, a higher-ranking one beats a lower-ranking one. A three-card sequence is worth 20, a four-card one 50, five 100, six 150, seven 200, eight 250, nine 300. The sequence order – Ace, King, Queen, Jack, Ten, Nine, Eight, Seven and Six, is the same in every suit, including trumps. A longer sequence beats a shorter one. If equal in length, a higher-ranking one beats a lower-ranking one. A Marriage between the King and Queen of trumps, a *Stöck*, is worth 20.

PLAY

The player to the dealer's left leads to the first trick. If the lead is a trump, the other players must follow suit, unless the only trump a player is holding is the Jack of trumps. In this case, any card may be played. If a plain suit is led, the others are free to follow suit or trump. In neither case can a lower trump be played if a higher one has already been led, unless a player's hand consists of nothing but trumps, in which case any card can be played.

SCORING

The highest-scoring card is the Jack of trumps (the *Puur*), worth 20 points, followed by the Nine of trumps (the *Näll*), which scores 14. Aces score 11, Kings four, Queens three, the other Jacks two and Tens 10. The other Nines, together with the Eights, Sevens and Sixes, do not score.

At the end of a hand, the two players taking the most meld points each score a game point. If scores are drawn, the pack is cut to break the tie. A player scoring less than 21 meld points is penalized by having a game point taken away. Game points are sometimes called 'sticks' and minus points are 'potatoes'.

Left: If two players tie at the end of a hand for the second-best score in meld points, the players concerned cut the pack and whoever draws the highest card scores the game point.

CONCLUSION

A player drops out on reaching either five game points or seven sticks, depending on which version of the game is being played. The last player left in is the loser.

SCHIEBER JASS

Schieber is probably the most popular member of the Swiss Jass family of card games. The game itself is a variant of Handjass, although its precise rules vary. It is played with a 36-card Jass pack, but here the suits of Acorns, Flowers, Shields and Bells have been substituted with the English counterparts Clubs, Spades, Hearts and Diamonds, respectively.

OBJECT

To win 3,000 points in total, by melding (matching sets of cards) and winning tricks.

THE DEAL

From the 36 card-deck, each player gets nine cards dealt in threes. The holder of the 7♠ starts the bidding, leads to the first trick and deals the second hand.

BIDDING AND CONTRACTS

The player holding the 7♠ can choose which contract is to be played, or can decide to *schieben* (shove) the responsibility over to his partner. The choice is between suit contracts in Clubs and Spades, which score single; Hearts or Diamonds, which score double; and the no-trump contracts (*Obenabe* – meaning literally 'top-down' – and *Undenufe* – meaning 'bottom-up'), which score treble.

PLAY

The player to the dealer's left leads. If the lead is a trump, the other players must follow suit, unless the only trump a player is holding is the Jack of trumps. In this case, any card may be played. If a plain suit is led, the others are free to follow suit or trump. In neither case can a lower trump be played if a higher one has already been led, unless a player's hand consists of nothing but trumps, in which case any card can be played.

In a no-trump contract, players must follow suit if they can. Each player announces the highest *Weis* (meld) he holds when he plays to the first trick. The partnership with the highest *Weis* scores for it, and for any other *Weis* that it may hold, the score being multiplied by the factor for the contract. Their opponents score nothing. A player holding the King and Queen of trumps may announce '*Stöck*' ('Marriage') as the second card is played.

You will need: 52-card deck with Fives and below removed

Card ranking: *Obenabe* ('top-down') no-trumps contracts: Eights (highest), Sevens, Sixes, Nines, Tens, Jacks, Queens, Kings and Aces. *Undenufe* ('bottom-up') no-trumps contracts: Sixes (highest), Sevens, Eights, Nines, Tens, Jacks, Queens, Kings and Aces. Plain suit contracts: Jacks (highest), Nines, Aces, Kings, Queens, Tens, Eights, Sevens and Sixes

Players: Four, in partnerships of two

Ideal for: 14+

SCORING

In *Obenabe* contracts Aces are worth 11 points, Kings four, Queens three, Jacks two, Tens 10 and Eights eight. Nines, Sevens and Sixes count for nothing. In *Undenufe* contracts, Sixes score 11, Eights eight, Tens 10, Jacks two, Queens three and Kings four. Sevens, Nines and Aces do not score. In plain suit contracts, Jacks score 20, Nines 14, Aces 11, Kings four, Queens three and Tens 10. The other cards are valueless.

After each hand, both partnerships multiply their totals by the factor for the hand. The first partnership to score 3,000 points wins. If the losing partnership has failed to score more than 1,500, the winners are awarded a bonus game. If a side claims a win during the first trick of a hand, their opponents can counter-claim. *Stöck* (Marriage) is scored, followed by *Weis* (meld) and *Stich* (first trick), to establish who won first. Twenty points are awarded for *Stöck* (Marriage), which again is multiplied by the factor for the contract. The winner of the last trick scores a bonus of five points. If either side manages to take all nine tricks, a bonus of 100 for 'match' is awarded.

Left: In an *Undenufe* contract, the meld that contains higher trick winners is the winning three-card sequence. In this instance, 6-7-8 is the higher and Queen-King-Ace the lower meld.

CONCLUSION

A hand continues until all tricks have been taken. The game lasts until one partnership or the other scores at least 3,000 points – this typically takes 12 hands.

8 | CANASTA GAMES

ALTHOUGH THEY ARE MEMBERS OF THE RUMMY GENRE, CANASTA GAMES HAVE ONE IMPORTANT DIFFERENCE. INSTEAD OF USING MELDS (MATCHES) SIMPLY AS A TOOL FOR GETTING RID OF CARDS IN HAND, PLAYERS SCORE POSITIVELY FOR THE MELDS THEMSELVES. CANASTA ITSELF WAS THE MOST POPULAR AMERICAN CARD GAME OF THE 1950s. IT REACHED THE USA FROM LATIN AMERICA IN ABOUT 1948, AND IS STILL PLAYED BY MILLIONS AROUND THE WORLD.

In fact, Canasta – the word is Spanish for 'basket' – was not the first game to introduce a positive scoring system for melds. The honour belongs to a game called Michigan Rum and another called 500 Rummy, both of which were widely played in the 1920s and 1930s. However, Canasta certainly has been the most influential worldwide. Although it is invariably regarded as a partnership game, perhaps because Bridge players invented it, it works just as well for two players.

The story of Canasta goes back to 1939, when well-to-do attorney Segundo Santos and his architect friend Alberto Serrato met in the Jockey Club of Montevideo, Uruguay, to devise an alternative to Bridge. The new game quickly spread throughout South America and then, after the Second World War, to the USA. It was soon played everywhere, from smart resorts on the eastern seaboard to highly fashionable clubs in California. American forces overseas spread the game to Asia, Europe and even the Soviet Union, and for a time in the early 1950s, it came close to displacing Contract Bridge as the world's most popular card game.

The various games Canasta has spawned over the years all have their individual quirks. In Samba, for instance, three packs of cards are used. Hand and Foot is another interesting variant, in which each player is dealt two sets of cards: the hand and the foot.

Above: Originating in Uruguay, Canasta reached dizzying heights of popularity in the USA in the early 1950s.

SAMBA

There are seemingly countless variations on classic Canasta. Some are simple adaptations to suit differing numbers of players, while others have developed into interesting games in their own right. Of these, Samba – also known as Samba-Canasta and, in the Netherlands, as Straat-Canasta (Sequence Canasta) – has been the most influential.

OBJECT

To be the first player to score 10,000 points by melding (matching sets of cards) in order to win the game.

THE DEAL

With two to five players, the deal is 15 cards to each player; six players get 13 cards each. The remaining cards form the stock, the top card of which is turned up to start the discard pile.

Left: Samba is characterized by allowing same-suit sequences as melds, as well as groups. A sequence, however, is not allowed to contain any wild cards.

MELDS

Same-suit sequences and groups are allowed. A group of seven or more cards is a *Canasta* and a seven-card sequence is a *Samba*. To go out, a player or partnership must have melded at least two *Canastas*, two *Sambas* or one of each. Wild cards – Jokers and Twos – cannot be used in a sequence, while a group may contain only two.

Aces and wild cards count for 20 points, Kings to Eights 10, and Sevens to Fours and black Threes five. Red Threes can be melded only if two *Sambas* or *Canastas* have already been laid, in which case each is worth 100 bonus points (1,000 if all six are melded).

If any are left in hand, they count as 750 penalty points. Black Threes can be melded in groups, but only when going out. Wild cards and Threes block the discard pile if discarded. Using the top card, which is blocking it, to start a new meld, unblocks it.

You will need: Three 52-card decks; six Jokers; scorecards

Card ranking: Ace down to Four, with Twos and Jokers serving as wild cards, and Threes having special rules attached to them (see 'Play' for wild cards and Threes)

Players: Two to six. If there are two, three or five, they play independently; if four or six, they play in partnerships

Ideal for: 14+

PLAY

Each player draws two cards from the stock, melds if he can, and discards a card. To use the discard pile, players must hold two natural cards of the same rank as the top discard, or, if they have not yet melded, meet the initial meld requirements. For scores under 1,500 points, this means the cards must be worth 50 points; for up to 3,000, 90 points; for up to 6,000, 120 points and for 7,000 or more 150 points.

SCORING AND CONCLUSION

Scores are calculated by taking the value of the cards that have been melded and deducting from that the value of cards left in hand. Any bonus points are then added. Each *Samba* is worth 1,500 points. A pure *Canasta* – one made up solely of natural cards – scores 500 and a mixed one 300. Going out is worth 200 points. The first to score 10,000 points wins outright.

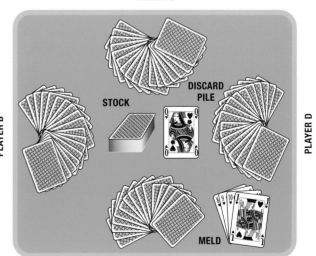

Above: Having already laid down a meld in Hearts, Player A can pick up the discard pile and add the Q♥ to the meld. Had the meld been in hand rather than laid to the table, Player A could not then have picked up the discard pile.

CANASTA

Invented in 1939 in Uruguay, Canasta is one of the great successes of modern card games. The rules vary, but always include laying at least one seven-card meld (matching set) or *Canasta*.

OBJECT

To make melds – three cards or more of the same rank other than Jokers, Twos and Threes – and build them up into *Canastas*, which are melds of at least seven cards.

THE DEAL

Each player is dealt 11 cards singly, after which the remaining cards are placed face down to form the stock. Its top card is turned face up to start the discard pile. If the turn-up is a Joker, Two or a red Three – Jokers and Twos are wild cards (that is, they can represent any card) – another card is turned up and placed on top of it. A player dealt one or more red Threes must place them face up in front of him and draw replacements from the stock. They are bonus cards that take no part in play.

Left: When a red Three tops the discard pile it is placed at right angles over it, meaning it is frozen and no player can take the pile. To unfreeze the pile, a player needs to have two natural cards of the same rank as the turn-up in hand.

Right: Black Threes are stop cards. When one tops the discard pile, the pile cannot be picked up until the Three is covered by another card. They cannot be melded unless a player is 'going out', (getting rid of all cards in hand).

You will need: Two 52-card decks; four Jokers; scorecards

Card ranking: Ace down to Four, with Twos and Jokers serving as wild cards, and Threes having special rules attached to them (see 'Play' for wild cards and Threes)

Players: Four, in partnerships of two

Ideal for: 14+

MELDS

Suits are irrelevant in Canasta, so melds consist of three or more cards of the same rank. At least two of these cards must be natural cards as opposed to wild ones. No meld can contain more than three wild cards, although there is no limit to the number of natural cards in one.

If a seven-card meld is all natural, it is termed a natural *Canasta*. If it contains wild cards, it is mixed. Adding a wild card to extend a natural *Canasta* will turn it into a mixed one, but a wild card cannot be shifted from meld to meld. Nor is a partnership allowed to run more than one meld of a given rank or to add cards to a meld laid by the opposing side.

The first meld laid by a partnership must meet or beat a specific points requirement, which is calculated according to that partnership's current score. At the start of play, it is 50 points. If a partnership's score is 1,500 or over, it is 90 points and, if 3,000 or more, it is 120.

INDIVIDUAL CARD SCORES:

- Red Threes – 100 points each.
- Jokers – 50 points each.
- Aces and Twos – 20 points each.
- Kings, Queens, Jacks, Tens to Eights – 10 points each.
- Sevens, Sixes, Fives, Fours and black Threes – five points each.

Left: At the start of play, the value of cards in a first meld must be at least 50 points. The far left meld is unacceptable, as Jacks are only worth 10 points. Aces score 20, so the second meld could be laid.

Right: Twos and Jokers in Canasta serve as wild cards, that is, they can represent any card.

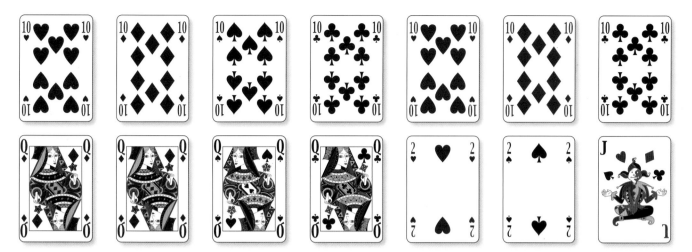

Above: The natural *Canasta* is worth 500 bonus points, plus 70 points as it is comprised of Tens. The mixed *Canasta* is worth 300 bonus points plus a further 130: 10 each for the Queens, 20 each for the Twos and 50 for the Joker.

PLAY

At the start of a turn, the player concerned can draw the top card of the stock or take the discard pile in its entirety. If the player chooses the first option, the card can be added to hand, melded or, if desired, discarded at the end of the turn. The second option applies only if the top discard can be melded at once. Nor may the discard pile be taken if the top discard is a wild card or a black Three. The latter is a stop card. By discarding one, a player can stop an opponent taking the pile until the Three is covered by another card. Moreover, black Threes cannot be melded unless a player is 'going out' – that is, getting rid of all cards in hand.

If the turn-up is a wild card or a red Three, no player can take the pile. It is what is termed 'frozen'. Nor may a partnership take it if it has yet to meld. To unfreeze the pile, a player needs to have two natural cards of the same rank as the turn-up in hand. The three cards can then be used to make a new meld, or be added to an existing one. Players end their turns by making a discard face up to the discard pile. This can be any card except a red Three.

CONCLUSION AND SCORING

Play ends when a player goes out, which can be by melding, laying off, or discarding the last card in hand, provided that the partnership concerned has laid at least one *Canasta*. Each partnership scores the value of the cards it has melded, plus bonuses of 500 points for each natural *Canasta*, 300 for each mixed one and 100 for each red Three declared (800 if all four red Threes are held). There is a further bonus of 100 points for going out, which is doubled if the player is going out 'concealed' – that

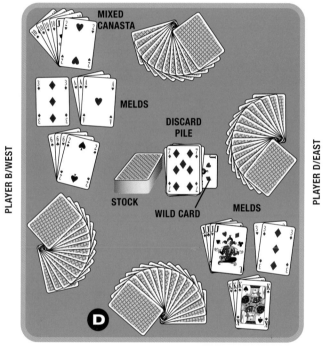

Above: A game of Canasta in progress. The North–South partnership is well on its way to a mixed *Canasta* in Tens, and also has melds in Sixes and Aces, together with a red Three. East–West has two red Threes, and melds in Jacks and Kings. The discard pile is currently frozen by a wild card, meaning that no player can pick up the pile unless he holds in his hand two cards of the same rank as the card topping the discard pile (here, a Seven).

is, without having previously made any melds or lay-offs and doing so by playing a complete *Canasta*.

The value of cards left in hand is subtracted from both totals. If a partnership has failed to lay a single meld, or failed to declare a red Three, each red Three it may hold counts for 100 points against it (800 points if all four are held). The cumulative score needed to win the game is 5,000 points, the margin of victory being the difference between the scores of the two partnerships.

HAND AND FOOT

Invented in North America, this fascinating game has several features that set it apart from other games of its ilk. It uses one more pack than the number of players – up to five can play – plus Jokers. Each player is dealt two separate hands simultaneously and there are three types of combinations – natural, mixed and wild. The last of these consists entirely of Jokers and Twos.

OBJECT

To meld (group) as many cards as possible and either to go out first or to be left with as little 'deadwood' (cards that are not in any meld) as possible. You score points for cards you have melded, and lose points for any cards left in your hand at the end of the play.

THE DEAL

Once it has been agreed which partnership is to deal first and after the cards have been thoroughly shuffled, one partner takes part of the deck and deals four stacks of 13 cards face down from it. This is the Hand. Meanwhile, the partner of the hand dealer does the same with the other part of the deck until each player has a second stack, known as the Foot. The remaining cards are placed face down to form the stock, the top card of which is turned up and placed next to it to start the discard pile. If the turn-up is a red Three or a wild card – a Two or a Joker – it is buried in the stock and the next card turned up.

Above: A feature of Hand and Foot is that matching combinations, known as melds, can consist entirely of wild cards, which are Twos and Jokers.

You will need: Five 52-card decks plus ten Jokers, for four players; scorecards

Card ranking: Ace down to Four, with Twos and Jokers serving as wild cards (see 'Play', opposite, for rules on this and Threes)

Players: Ideally, four, in partnerships of two

Ideal for: 14+

PLAYER C

FOOT · HAND

HAND · FOOT

PLAYER B · PLAYER D

STOCK · DISCARD PILE

FOOT · HAND

HAND · FOOT

D

PLAYER A

Above: After shuffling the packs, one partner takes part of the deck, deals four face-down stacks of 13 cards and passes them around the table in a clockwise direction until each player has a stack – the Hand. Meanwhile, the dealer's partner takes another part of the deck and deals a further four stacks of 13 cards each, once again passing these in a clockwise direction until each player has a second stack – the Foot.

MELDING

Players score points for the cards that they have melded and lose points for any cards left in hand at the end of play. In this game, a meld is a set of from three to seven cards of the same rank. Once such a meld has been started, either partner is at liberty to add more cards to it until there are seven in place.

There are three valid melds. A natural (or clean) meld contains no wild cards, while a mixed (or dirty) meld contains one or two. There must be at least six cards in such a meld for two wild cards to be included. A wild meld, as its name implies, consists entirely of wild cards. A complete meld of seven cards is called a pile.

PLAY

Players pick up and play the Hand first. The Foot stays face down sight unseen until its owner has played the last card from the Hand. Before each player plays, he must place any red Threes held in the Hand face up and draw replacements from the stock. The player to the left of the person who dealt the hands plays first.

Each player starts by drawing the top two cards from the stock. He then melds some cards or adds to his partner's melds and finally discards one card face up to the discard pile. An alternative to drawing from the stock is to pick up the top seven cards from the discard pile. This option is open only if the top discard is not a Three, and the player is holding two cards of the same rank as the top discard that can be melded with it immediately.

The first meld each partnership makes in each round must meet the minimum meld requirements. Several melds may be made at once to achieve this. In the first round, the requirement is at least 50 points, in the second 90, in the third 120, and in the fourth 150. Jokers are worth 50 points each, Twos and Aces 20, Kings down to Eights 10, and Sevens to Fours score five points.

Neither red nor black Threes may be melded. Red Threes, if declared, are worth a bonus 100 points each, but any left in hand count for 100 penalty points. If discarded, black Threes block the discard pile, so they are often used tactically. Any left in hand count for five penalty points. This means discarding any Threes held in hand one at a time on to the discard pile as quickly as possible.

Below: An excellent, if unlikely, opening hand. The red Three can be declared, earning a bonus of 100 points, while the black Three can be saved to block the discard pile at an opportune moment. The wild Twos and Jokers can be used towards a wild meld, or towards a mixed meld in Queens or Aces.

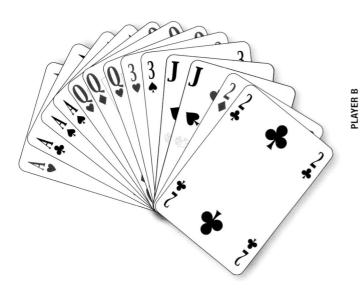

SCORING AND CONCLUSION

For a player to be allowed to go out, the partnership concerned must have melded two natural, two mixed and one wild meld between them. The other partner must have picked up his Foot and played at least part of a turn from it. The player seeking to go out must also have obtained his partner's permission to do so.

Scores are then totalled, points deducted for cards left in hand, and bonuses awarded. Each natural pile is worth 500 points, a mixed one 300 and a wild pile 1,500. This is why most players, if possible, try to complete this particular pile as soon as they can. There is an additional 100-point bonus for going out.

If the stock is depleted to the point where no player can draw from it, play also ends, although it may be possible to continue for a time as long as each player is able to take and meld the previous player's discard. In this case, both partnerships score for the cards that they have melded, less the points for the cards they have remaining in their Hands and Feet. Obviously, the bonus for going out is not awarded.

The game ends when a partnership has made 10,000 points, or the four rounds have been played. In that case, the partnership winning the most rounds wins the game.

Below: Here, only Player A's hand is shown, along with the table cards. Players A and C have a natural meld of Aces and are well on the way to completing a mixed meld in Queens. Their opponents have nearly completed a wild meld and have started a mixed meld in Nines. Player A, whose turn it is to play, can pick up the discarded J♠ or pick up two cards from the top of the stock.

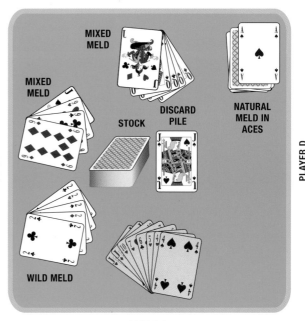

PENNIES FROM HEAVEN

This variant of Canasta is notable for the highly unusual role played by Sevens. They may not be discarded until each partnership has grouped seven or more cards consisting solely of Sevens. Nor may they be discarded when going out. There are also two deals in this game.

OBJECT

To score points by melding (grouping) cards into four types of *Canastas* (a meld of seven or more cards): natural, mixed, wild and sevens. A team needs one of each of these types to go out.

THE DEAL

Each player receives 13 cards, dealt singly, and followed by a packet of 11 cards, which is kept face down until a player has personally completed a *Canasta* by laying the requisite seventh card from his hand.

The second hand, the so-called 'pennies from heaven', can then be picked up and taken into hand. The remaining cards form the stock, the top card of which is turned up to start the discard pile.

You will need: Four 52-card decks; eight Jokers; scorecards

Card ranking: Aces down to Eights, then Sixes, Fives and Fours, with Twos and Jokers serving as wild cards, and Threes and Sevens having special rules attached to them (see 'Play' for wild cards and Threes)

Players: Four or six, playing in partnerships

Ideal for: 14+

Left: A *Canasta* of Sevens in Pennies from Heaven scores 1,500 points.

MELDS AND CANASTAS

A natural *Canasta* – consisting of seven cards of the same rank with no wild cards – is worth a bonus of 500 points. A mixed one, containing up to three wild cards with all the others of the same rank, counts for 300. A *Canasta* of seven wild cards scores 1,000 points and a *Canasta* made up of Sevens scores 1,500 points.

A meld must consist of a minimum of three cards and a maximum of seven. Depending on a partnership's cumulative score, the first meld to be laid must meet a minimum points requirement. For a minus score, this is 15 points; for a score from zero to 4,995, it is 50 points; and for one from 5,000 to 9,995, it is 90 points. If the score is between 10,000 and 14,995, the requirement is 120 points and 150 thereafter.

A mixed meld in process of construction must contain at least two natural cards and not more than three wild ones. A natural meld can be turned into a mixed one by adding wild cards to it, while, once a meld has been completed, the partnership that melded can start another meld of the same rank.

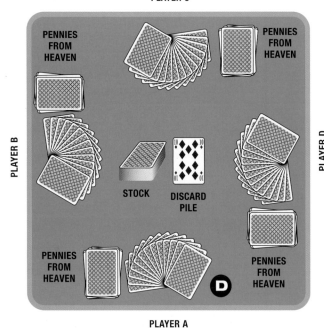

Above: Each player is dealt a batch of 11 cards in addition to his main hand of 13 cards. The second hand cannot be picked up until a player has personally completed a *Canasta* by laying the requisite seventh card from hand.

PLAY

Each player in turn has the option of drawing the top two cards from the stock or taking the entire discard pile. He can then start a new meld or add cards to melds his

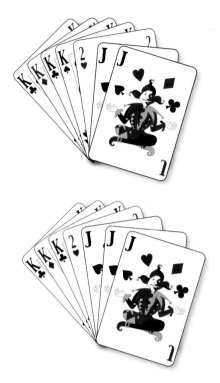

Above: The meld at the top is acceptable, containing no more than three wild cards. The second of the two contains four, so would not be allowed.

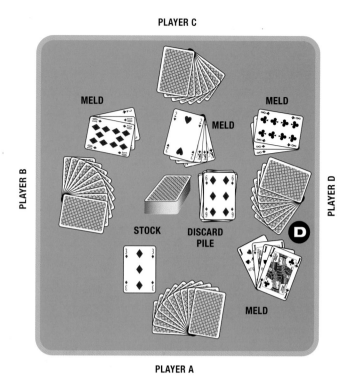

Above: An example of play in progress. Player A has laid down a red Three (and drawn a replacement from the stock) and a meld of Jacks. Player B has begun a meld in Tens, Player C one in Kings, and Player D has, so far, a natural meld in Eights.

partnership has already started constructing. To end a turn, one card from hand is discarded face up on to the discard pile. Whether the discard pile can be taken or not is subject to certain conditions. If its top card is a natural one and the player concerned holds two matching natural cards in hand, the pile may be taken, always provided that the three cards are melded immediately and that the minimum meld requirement has been satisfied previously. It can also be taken if its top card matches an existing meld of fewer than seven cards, provided that it is added immediately to that meld. A discarded wild card freezes the pile.

Twos and Jokers are wild cards. Jokers are worth 50 points each, Twos and Aces 20 points, Kings down to Eights 10, and Sevens to black Threes score five points. Red and black Threes have the same properties as in regular Canasta. Any player who is dealt or draws a red Three must place it face up on the table immediately and draw a replacement from the stock.

Each declared red Three counts for 100 bonus points (1,000 if the same partnership lays out all eight of them). Any left in hand score 100 penalties each (1,000 if all eight are held). Black Threes cannot be melded, except by a player going out. If one is discarded, it blocks the discard pile, as does a red Three if that is the first card to be turned up after the deal.

SCORING

A partnership must have completed all four types of *Canasta* before one of its players can go out by melding all of the remaining cards in hand, or all bar one of them, which is the final discard. This must not be a Seven. It is customary to ask a partner's permission to go out before doing so, in which case the player concerned must abide by that partner's decision.

The partnerships each score all the cards they have melded, plus any bonuses for *Canastas* and a further 100-point bonus for the side that went out first. From this, they deduct the value of any cards left in hand. Scores for red Threes are added or debited as appropriate.

CONCLUSION

If the stock is exhausted, play can continue as long as the players are willing to pick up discards. If not, it ends and the hand is scored as above, although the bonus for going out is obviously not awarded. The first partnership to score 20,000 or more points wins the game. If the scores are tied, a deciding hand is played.

PINÁCULO

This game originated in Spain and is regarded by some as a forerunner of Canasta. Jokers and Twos are wild cards. As well as scoring for groupings (melds) in the same way as Canasta, there are additional scores for specified melds.

OBJECT

To score 1,500 points over as many deals as it takes, scoring extra for melds and conceding penalties for 'deadwood', or cards not in a meld.

THE DEAL

After the initial shuffle, the player to the dealer's left cuts the cards. Each player is then dealt 11 cards singly from the bottom half of the cut pack. The remaining cards are stacked face down to form the stock, and the top card is turned up to start the discard pile. If exactly the right number of cards (44) is cut for the deal, the cutter scores a 50-point bonus.

MELDING

A meld contains three or more cards of the same rank, or three or more in suit and sequence. The latter is an *Escalera* and must contain at least two natural (not wild) cards. In addition, Aces count as high and Threes low.

Melds are the property of the player or partnership that played them, and must be kept separate. No two melds may be combined, even if their ranks match or such a combination will complete a sequence.

You will need: Two 52-card decks; four Jokers; scorecards

Card ranking: Standard, with Twos and Jokers being wild

Players: Four, in partnerships of two

Ideal for: 14+

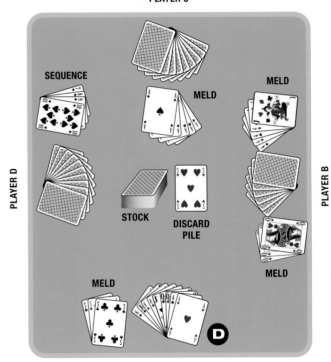

Above: Player A can play the J♠ and 6♠ on to Player D's sequence, the A♥ on to Player C's meld and the 4♣ and Q♣ on to Player B's melds. But first, he must decide whether to pick up the 5♥, together with the rest of the discard pile, adding the Five to his existing meld, or to pick up from the stock.

Left: The highest-scoring meld in Pináculo, 11 of a kind, is called a *Pinnacle* and scores either 3,000 points or 1,500 points, depending on whether it was constructed gradually or not.

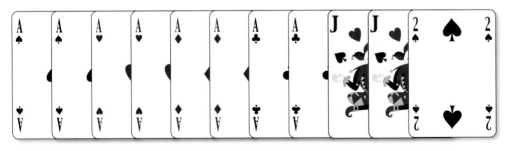

Left: The lowest-scoring meld in Pináculo is five court cards and a wild card, which scores 120 points.

PLAY

The player to the right of the dealer leads and play proceeds in an anti-clockwise direction. Each player in turn draws a card from the stock or takes the whole discard pile. The player then goes on to start a meld or to lay off cards to a meld that has already been started by the partnership. At the end of each turn, a card is discarded face up to the discard pile.

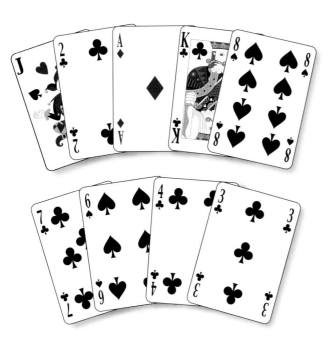

Above: The penalty points for being left with these two sets of cards contrast sharply. In the first set, the Joker would count for 30 points, the Two for 20, the Ace for 15, and the King and Eight for 10 each, making a total of 85. In the second, each card counts for just five points, making a total of 20.

If a player is holding a natural card that is being represented by a wild card at either end of an incomplete *Escalera*, he may substitute a natural card for the wild one. The wild card is not taken into his hand, but is placed sideways at one end of the *Escalera* as a reminder to score it at the end of play. There is an added twist. A partnership or player with 750 points is said to be *barbelé* (French for caught in the barbed wire). This means that the next meld they lay must be worth at least 70 points. Any meld lower than this must be withdrawn and the offending partnership has to concede a 50-point penalty.

SCORING

Players score positively for cards in melds but lose points for cards left in hand at the end of the game. Jokers score 30 points either way, Twos 20, Aces 15, Kings to Eights 10 and Sevens to Threes five points each.

Scores are calculated at the end of the game. There are points for melds and bonus or penalty points scored during play: there is a bonus of 20 for going out; going out without the use of a wild card doubles the values of all the cards in the final meld; going out 'concealed' (melding all 11 cards) similarly doubles their face values; if they are all natural cards, their values are quadrupled.

SCORING MELDS

Specific melds score a premium number of points, rather than their face value, as follows:

- A *Pinnacle* (a meld of 11 of a kind, declared simultaneously) scores 3,000 points; a *Pinnacle* constructed gradually in one hand scores 1,500 points.
- A clean *Escalera* (a sequence of 11 natural cards in suit) scores 1,000 points.
- An unclean *Escalera* (containing a Two of a matching suit) scores 800 points.
- An unclean *Escalera* (containing two Twos of a matching suit) scores 750 points.
- A dirty *Escalera* (that is, one containing one or more non-matching Twos) scores 550.
- A meld of eight natural Aces scores 1,000 points.
- A meld of eight natural Kings, Queens or Jacks scores 750 points.
- A meld of seven natural Aces scores 400 points.
- A meld of seven natural Kings, Queens or Jacks scores 300.
- A meld of six natural Aces scores 300 points.
- A meld of six natural court cards scores 200 points.
- A meld of six Aces that includes a wild card scores 180 points.
- A meld of six court cards that includes a wild card scores 120 points.

Eight natural number cards score their total face value plus 50. Each Joker replaced by a natural card during the course of play scores an extra 30 points. Each Two that was similarly replaced scores an additional 15 in an *Escalera* or twice face value in a meld of cards of the same rank.

CONCLUSION

When a player has one card left in hand, he must call '*Pumba!*' or be penalized 50 points. The game ends when a player goes out by melding or laying off the remaining cards in hand, with or without discarding. It also ends if the stock is exhausted.

CONTINENTAL RUMMY

There are many different versions of this attractive game, which can be played by up to 12 at a time. What makes Continental Rummy different from other games of its ilk is that no groupings (melds) can be laid until a player can go out by doing so. No cards may be laid off, nor can natural cards be exchanged for wild ones.

You will need: Two packs or more, with Jokers. Five players or fewer use a double pack plus two Jokers; six to eight use a triple pack with three Jokers; more than nine use a quadruple pack with four Jokers; gambling chips/counters

Card ranking: Aces rank high and low, the remaining cards ranking from Kings down to Threes; Twos and Jokers are wild cards

Players: Two to 12

Ideal for: 10+

OBJECT

To meld all one's cards in sequences of the same suit and in only one of the specified patterns, which are 3–3–3–3–3, 3–4–4–4 or 3–3–4–5 (see picture, below).

THE DEAL

If two packs are used, the dealer shuffles. Otherwise, the dealer and another player each shuffle parts of the pack – the dealer has the right to shuffle second, and these packs are then combined. Each player is dealt 15 cards three at a time, the remainder being placed face down to form the stock. In some versions of the game, the dealer is awarded a bonus of 15 chips for lifting off exactly the right number of cards to complete the deal. The top card of the stock is turned up to start the discard pile. Players are given an agreed number of gambling chips.

PLAY

Each player in turn draws either the top card of the stock or the turn-up from the discard pile and then discards one of his cards. Only same-suit sequences count, not matched sets. To go out means melding five three-card sequences, three four-card and one three-card sequences, or one five-card, one four-card and two three-card ones. Two or more of these sequences may be of the same suit, but a sequence must not 'go round the corner' – that is, an Ace can count as high or low, but not as both.

SCORING

If a player goes out without drawing a single card, there is a bonus of ten chips; for going out after only drawing once, seven chips; and for doing so without playing a Joker or a Two, 10 chips. Melding all 15 cards of the same suit is also worth 10 extra chips.

CONCLUSION

The game ends when a player melds 15 cards in one of the specified patterns and makes a final discard. The winner collects a chip from each of the other players for winning, two for each melded Joker and one for each Two.

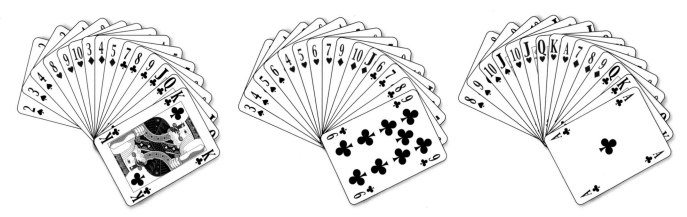

Above: The sequences in Continental Rummy must conform to specified patterns, comprising: five sets of same-suit sequences of three; three sets of four and one of three; or two sets of three, together with one of four and one of five. Sequences must be of the same suit, and they must not 'go round the corner' – in other words, a sequence could not run from King through to Two.

500 Rum

This variant of Rummy dates from the 1930s. In it, points are scored for grouped (melded) cards and lost for unmelded ones. Unlike similar games, players are not limited to only taking the top discard: more cards may be drawn, but at least one must be laid off or melded straight away.

Object

To score points by melding cards, the game being won by the first player to score 500 or more points.

The Deal

Players draw for deal, and the person with the lowest card deals first. Each player is dealt seven cards. If only two are playing, the deal is 13 cards each, and the remaining cards form the stock. The top card of the stock is then turned face up to start the discard pile. As play progresses, this should be spread sufficiently for players to see all the cards in it.

You will need: 52 cards (two packs for five or more players); no Jokers; scorecards

Card ranking: Aces high or low, then Kings down to Twos

Players: Two to eight, but three is optimal

Ideal for: 10+

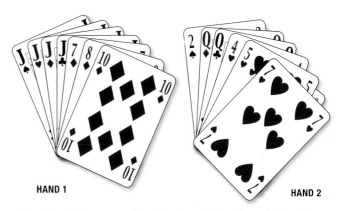

HAND 1   **HAND 2**

Above: To calculate scores, the point values of the cards each player has melded are added up and that of any cards left in hand are subtracted. The first hand here scores 40 points for the meld of four Jacks, but loses 25 points for the number cards, making a total of 15 points. The second hand scores 22 points for the same-suit sequence in Hearts, but loses 22 points for the two Queens and 2♠, meaning that no points are scored.

Play

Each player in turn draws the top card of the stock or any card from the discard pile. In the latter case, the desired card must be played immediately, and all the cards lying above it must be taken. The other cards may be melded or laid off in the same turn or added to the hand.

Melds consist of sets of three or four cards of the same rank and sequences of three or more cards of the same suit. Sequences may not 'go round the corner', in other words, a sequence of Ace, King, and Queen is valid, but King, Ace, and Two is not. Each player finishes by discarding a card.

Scoring and Conclusion

Play ends when a player goes out – that is, gets rid of all the cards in his hand, or the stock is exhausted. To calculate scores, the point values of the cards each player has melded are added up and that of any cards left in hand are subtracted. An Ace is worth 15 points if high and a single point if low. The court cards count for 10 points each and the number cards at face value.

The first player to score 500 points wins the game, the winning margin being the difference between that and the final scores of the other players.

PLAYER C

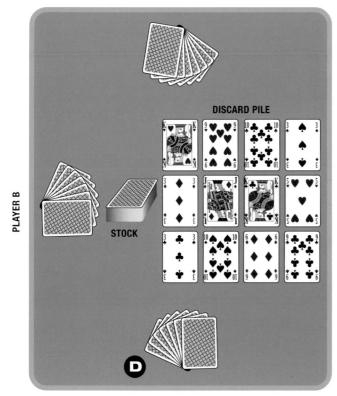

PLAYER B

DISCARD PILE

STOCK

D

PLAYER A

Above: The discard pile in 500 Rum should be spread out, so that all the cards in it can be seen by every player.

9 | VYING GAMES

IN THIS GROUP OF GAMES, OF WHICH POKER IN ALL ITS FORMS IS UNQUESTIONABLY THE BEST KNOWN AND THE MOST POPULAR, PLAYERS BET ON WHO HOLDS THE BEST HAND. MOST GAMES END WITH A 'SHOWDOWN', IN WHICH THE HANDS ARE COMPARED TO SEE WHICH IS THE BEST. VYING GAMES ARE UNUSUAL IN THAT THERE IS NO ACTUAL CARD PLAY, ALTHOUGH PLAYERS OCCASIONALLY HAVE THE CHANCE TO IMPROVE THEIR HANDS BY DISCARDING AND DRAWING NEW CARDS.

As well as gambling, what these games have in common is that, to a greater or lesser extent, they all involve an element of bluff. This is why, although a player may be dealt a bad hand, he can still win by superior play. It means having the courage to bet on bad cards in the hope that the other players will lose their nerve and all drop out of play, so that you win by default. This happens when a player raises the stake and the others are not prepared to match the bet in case the stake-raising player has an unbeatable hand.

Vying can take either of two forms. In the first, the oldest type, players pay into a pot to back up the claim that they hold the best hand, or drop out, losing whatever they have staked. When only two players are left in the game, there is a showdown. The way to call this is by matching the previous player's stake. It does not have to be raised further.

In the second, newer form of vying, all the players in the game can force a showdown by matching the previous stake. This means that the player who previously raised the stake is unable to raise it further. The procedure for this can be quite complicated. In the Swedish game Chicago (not to be confused with the Bridge variant of the same name), there are two showdowns between the players before a final trick-taking phase.

Above: The film based on Fleming's *Casino Royale* features a game of no-limit Texas Hold 'em Poker between James Bond (Daniel Craig) and the chief villain.

POKER

It was in New Orleans in 1829 that the name Poker was first used for this game. Despite its somewhat insalubrious reputation, it has gone from strength to strength to become one of the world's most popular card games. What follows is an introduction to the basics, after which the most widely played Poker variations are covered individually.

OBJECT

To secure the best hand (in most forms of the game, this is the top combination of five cards) and win the pot, which holds all the bets made in any one deal).

PLAY

Between two to eight players can take part, but experts reckon five to eight is ideal. All players play individually and for themselves – there are no partnerships in Poker.

The game is played with a standard 52-card pack, sometimes with the addition of two Jokers, although some players prefer using two packs to speed up proceedings. If this option is preferred, the packs should be of contrasting colours.

If two hands are identical card for card, the hands are tied, since suits have no relative ranks in Poker. In such a case, the pot is split between the tied players.

SCORING

Poker is traditionally a gambling game, so winnings are settled up in gambling chips, which can be exchanged for money. If you wish to play Poker as a family game, it is still best to play for stakes, as this helps to concentrate the minds of the players and reduces the temptation to indulge in unrealistic bluffs. You can keep the stakes small and use alternatives to money.

POKER HANDS

From highest to lowest, poker hands rank as follows:

- Five of a Kind – Four Aces and Joker (obviously this can occur only in games where wild cards are being used).
- Royal Flush – A Straight Flush up to Ace.
- Straight Flush – A combined Straight and Flush; i.e. cards in sequence and of the same suit. A hand containing Ace, Two, Three, Four and Five is the second-highest Straight or Straight Flush, ranking between Ace, King, Queen, Jack and Ten and King, Queen, Jack, Ten and Nine.
- Four of a Kind – Four cards of the same face value (known as 'Quads').
- Full House – Three of a Kind ('Trips') and a Pair. When two players hold a Full House, the highest-ranking Trips wins.
- Flush – Five cards of the same suit. If another player holds a Flush, whoever holds the highest card wins.
- Straight – A sequence of five cards in any suit; e.g. 5♦, 6♣, 7♠, 8♥, 9♣. The highest Straight is one topped by an Ace, the lowest starts with an Ace. If two players hold a Straight, the one with the highest cards wins.
- Three of a Kind – Three cards of the same face value ('Trips'); e.g. Q♠, Q♣, Q♥.
- Two Pairs – Two sets of Pairs; e.g. 3♦, 3♥ and Q♠, Q♣. Whoever holds the highest card in the two hands (called the 'Kicker') wins, if two players hold matching Pairs of the same value.
- One Pair – Two cards of the same value; e.g. 3♦, 3♥ or Q♠, Q♣. If another player holds a Pair of the same value, then whoever holds the 'Kicker' wins.
- High card – A hand with no combination, but having within it the highest-ranking card among the hands in play.

Above: During a game, gambling chips are used to keep track of Poker winnings. Some argue it detaches players from the cash sums involved.

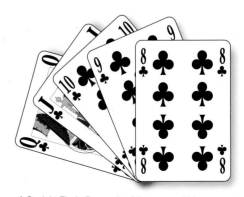

Above: A Straight Flush (five cards of the same suit) is a very strong Poker hand. If two players hold a Straight Flush, the highest card determines the winner.

HOW BETTING WORKS

The Banker

One player becomes the banker, issuing chips to each player before and during play. It is also his job to keep track of the bets.

The Ante

Depending on the game, players may have to put one or more chips into the pot to guarantee that there is something in the pot to generate competition. This is the ante.

The Stakes

To bet, players move chips from the stacks in front of them in turn towards the centre of the table, where they become part of the pot. These stakes, however, must be kept separate and not merged into a single pile, as it is essential to know exactly what each player has staked. Once a bet is made, it cannot be retracted.

Betting and Raising

There are normally two opportunities to bet – the first before the pot is opened and the second before a player opens the betting. Who is entitled to bet first varies between games, and depends on what rules are being played. It may depend, for instance, on what minimum card combination is required and on the smallest and highest amounts that are allowed as an opening bet. Regardless, the other players, starting with the player to the left of the one making the opening bet, have the chance to 'call' the bet by putting the same number of chips into the pot, or raising it.

A raise is one of the key elements of poker because it increases the cost to opponents of remaining in a hand, and also suggests that the player making one has a strong

Above: When betting, players should make their aims clear by announcing 'call' or 'raise' for example, and placing their chips immediately in front of them.

hand. Raising involves matching a previous bet and making an additional bet of at least equal value. For example, if the bet stands at 40 chips, anyone wishing to raise can expect to bet at least 80 chips – 40 to call the bet and a further 40 chips to increase the betting level.

Folding or Checking

The alternative is to fold or to check. In the former case, the folding player discards his hand and is out of the betting until the next deal. As players fold, they 'muck their hand' by placing their cards face down with the other discarded cards.

By checking when it is his turn to act, a player effectively defers a decision to bet, but remains in the hand. A player may check provided that no compulsory or voluntary bets have already been made during a betting round. If an opponent subsequently makes a bet, then a player who previously checked must choose whether to fold, call or raise when the action returns to him; he no longer has the option to check at this stage. A player who checks may subsequently raise a bet that has been raised by another player. This particular practice is called 'sandbagging or 'check-raising'.

Final Bets

Betting ends if all the players check, or when all the bets have been equalized, after which play continues, or there is a showdown, the result of which is that the player with the best hand wins the pot. If all the players fold by not calling the last raise, the last raiser wins the pot without having to show his hand.

Left: A game of Texas Hold 'em is underway in Caesar's Palace casino, Las Vegas, which is marketed as 'the entertainment capital of the world'.

WILD-CARD POKER

There are many different forms of Poker, but all of them can be played with one or more wild cards – that is, a card that its holder may count as any natural card missing from his hand. Their use increases the chances of making combinations, such as a Straight Flush or a Full House, and introduces an extra hand – Five of a Kind – into the game. Five of a Kind ranks the same as, or above, a Royal Flush.

The usual choices for wild cards start with Jacks, one or more of which may be added to the pack. If so, they are called 'bugs'. However, the extent of their wildness is limited by the rules. A Joker can stand for an Ace, a card of any suit for making a Flush, or a card of any rank or suit for making a Straight or Straight Flush.

DEUCES AND ONE-EYED JACKS

Twos are often played wild, especially in Deuces Wild, which is a popular form of Draw Poker. The J♠ and the J♥ – these are called One-eyed Jacks, because only one eye shows – are sometimes played as wild cards as well.

Which wild cards to use is down to prior agreement between the players. According to convention, if one wild card is agreed, it is a Joker and, for two, the One-eyed Jacks. For four, any four cards of a given rank are nominated and, for eight, any two ranks.

VARIABLE WILD CARDS

The more wild cards there are, the higher the winning hands. The game becomes even more complicated if variable wild cards are introduced.

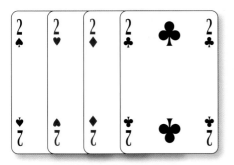

Left: Twos are often used as wild cards in Poker, especially in Deuces Wild, a popular form of Draw Poker.

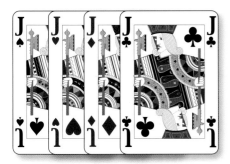

Left: When used as wild cards in Poker, Jacks are called 'bugs'. The J♠ and J♥ are called One-Eyed Jacks, because only one eye shows.

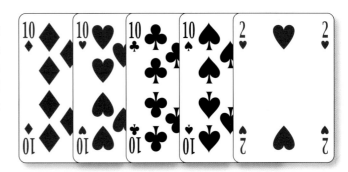

Above: If you are playing wild-card games, then an additional hand of Five of a Kind can come into play, which ranks the same as, or above, a Royal Flush and above a Straight Flush. Here, with Twos as wild cards, this hand counts as Five of a Kind.

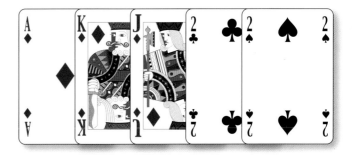

Above: It is wise to be clear on house rules when using wild cards. Here, for example, it ought to be decided whether a Royal Flush of an A♦, K♦ and J♦, plus any pair of Twos, substituting for the Q♦ and 10♦, count as the equal of a 'natural' Royal Flush or if it would be inferior to it.

In Five-Card Stud Poker, each player's hole card, that is the lowest card to be dealt face down, can be designated wild by its holder. In Seven-Card Stud, two cards are dealt face down and one face up. In Draw Poker, the hole card is the lowest card in a player's hand. If such a card is designated as wild, it means that every card of the same rank in its holder's hand is wild as well. It should be noted, though, that just because a card is wild in one player's hand, this does not make the same rank of card wild in the hands of other players.

Although wild cards do not alter the relative ranking of the hands, they do introduce a new one. This is Five of a Kind. In the event of two hands tying, the one with fewer wild cards in it wins. The most basic wild-card variant is Deuces Wild.

Draw Poker

Otherwise known as Five-Card Draw, this is the original form of the game. After the cards are dealt face down, players may decide to 'stand pat' or exchange cards. If the latter, they must discard the cards in hand before being dealt replacements.

Object

The object is to secure the best hand and thus win the pot (which holds all the bets that players have made in any one deal).

Buying In and The Ante

Before play starts, players must buy in to the game by buying an agreed number of chips from the banker. There should be at least 200 chips on hand.

White chips are the lowest, red chips are worth five whites and blue chips are worth four or five red chips. Each player antes (puts in) a chip to start the pot, or the dealer antes chips on his behalf.

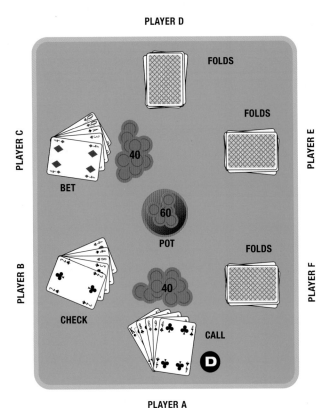

Above: After the deal, the player to the dealer's left (Player B) checks, since he does not hold a pair of Jacks. The option passes to Player C, who opens with a bet of 40 chips on the basis of his pair of Queens. Players D, E and F all fold, but Player A calls the bet.

You will need: 52-card deck, sometimes with the addition of two Jokers (some players prefer using two packs to speed up proceedings, in which case they should be of contrasting colours); gambling chips/counters

Card ranking: See box opposite

Players: Two to eight (experts consider five to eight is ideal)

Ideal for: 14+

The Deal

Once everyone has added an ante to the pot, players receive five cards, dealt face down singly clockwise around the table. Each player can discard up to three cards, after which the dealer deals the required number of replacements. Each player gets the chance to deal in turn.

Play
First Betting Round

Starting with the player to the dealer's left, each player has a chance to open the betting. A player must be holding a pair of Jacks or better to do this, a higher pair or a higher card combination. He must also be prepared to prove that he is entitled to open. The alternatives are to pass or to fold. If all players pass, the hands are thrown in and the pot is carried forward to the next deal.

Drawing

After the betting round is over, each player has the option of 'standing pat', that is, playing with the cards as dealt, or exchanging up to three cards. A player with an Ace may exchange four cards, provided that the Ace is first shown to the other players. The replacements are dealt from the top of the pack.

The cards are discarded face down, the player making the exchange announcing how many cards are being discarded. The dealer, who is always the last to draw, deals the requisite number of replacements immediately.

Second Betting Round

A second betting round follows, the first to speak this time being the player who initially opened the pot. Each player in turn may now check (which is indicated by knocking on the table) or bet. If all players check, the player who opened the pot originally must start the proceedings again. The other options are to call (that is, to match the previous stake), to raise or to fold.

Play ends when there are calls for a showdown, or if a time limit that has been agreed in advance is reached. If a player runs out of chips, he must buy more from the banker, or drop out. In the latter case, he forfeits any claim to the pot. The banker is nominated to keep the stock of chips and to record how many have been issued to each player, or how much each player has paid for his chips. A showdown may be called only after a raise.

CONCLUSION

In a showdown, the player with the best hand wins the pot. If all the other players have folded, however, the last player to have raised will automatically win without having to show his hand.

VARIANTS

Hi-Low Draw is probably the most common variant that can be played, where the holder of the highest and the lowest hands split the pot. In Lowball, which is popular in the western USA, the lowest hand wins. Aces are always low, so that two is the lowest possible Pair, while Straights and Flushes do not count. The lowest possible hand, known as a 'wheel' or a 'bicycle', consists of a Five, Four, Three, Two and an Ace, regardless of suits. In Double Draw, there is a second exchange of cards after the first betting round and then a further betting round.

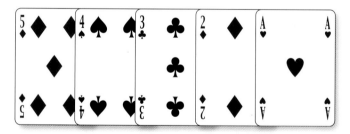

Above: In Lowball the lowest possible hand, known as a 'wheel' or a 'bicycle', consists of a Five, Four, Three, Two and an Ace, regardless of what the suit is.

SPECIAL HANDS

As well as introducing variants like the ones detailed above, many players also favour allowing so-called special hands into the game in addition to the standard ones. A Skip Straight, also known as a Dutch Straight, for instance, consists of five cards in alternate sequence, such as Queen, Ten, Eight, Six and Four. It beats Three of a Kind, but loses to a conventional Straight.

> ## POKER HANDS
>
> From highest to lowest, poker hands rank as follows:
>
> - Five of a Kind – Four Aces and Joker (obviously this can occur only in games where wild cards are being used).
> - Royal Flush – A Straight Flush up to Ace.
> - Straight Flush – A combined Straight and Flush; i.e. cards in sequence and of the same suit. A hand containing Ace, Two, Three, Four and Five is the second-highest Straight or Straight Flush, ranking between Ace, King, Queen, Jack and Ten and King, Queen, Jack, Ten and Nine.
> - Four of a Kind – Four cards of the same face value (known as 'Quads').
> - Full House – Three of a Kind ('Trips') and a Pair. When two players hold a Full House, the highest-ranking Trips wins.
> - Flush – Five cards of the same suit. If another player holds a Flush, whoever holds the highest card wins.
> - Straight – A sequence of five cards in any suit; e.g. 5♦, 6♣, 7♠, 8♥, 9♣. The highest Straight is one topped by an Ace, the lowest starts with an Ace. If two players hold a Straight, the one with the highest cards wins.
> - Three of a Kind – Three cards of the same face value ('Trips'); e.g. Q♠, Q♣, Q♥.
> - Two Pairs – Two sets of Pairs; e.g. 3♦, 3♥ and Q♠, Q♣. Whoever holds the highest card in the two hands (called the 'Kicker') wins, if two players hold matching Pairs of the same value.
> - One Pair – Two cards of the same value; e.g. 3♦, 3♥ or Q♠, Q♣. If another player holds a Pair of the same value, then whoever holds the 'Kicker' wins.
> - High card – A hand with no combination, but having within it the highest-ranking card among the hands in play.

A Round-the-Corner Straight is a sequence such as Three, Two, Ace, King and Queen, while a Bobtail is a four-card Flush or Straight with both ends open. Thus, Eight, Seven, Six and Five is a valid Bobtail, but Ace, King, Queen and Jack is not because only a single card, a Ten, can complete the sequence. A Bobtail beats a Pair, but loses to Two Pairs. If Bobtails are allowed, the player opening the pot can count holding one as the necessary qualification to do so. A Zebra is five cards that alternate in colour when put in numerical order.

Above: An example of a Round-the-Corner Straight.

Five-Card Stud

After Draw Poker, Five-Card Stud is the other classic form of the game with which non-poker players are most likely to be familiar. Its perceived benefit over the original draw or 'closed' form of the game derives from the fact that players receive most of their cards face up, giving them more information upon which to make betting decisions.

Object

To create the best-ranking hand, or bluff opponents into believing you have achieved this, so that at the showdown you take the pot.

The Deal

Players cut the pack to decide who deals, the role of dealer subsequently rotating on a clockwise basis. Participants in the game receive five cards during the course of each

You will need: 52 cards; Jokers optional; gambling chips/counters
Card ranking: See box below
Players: Any number up to eight
Ideal for: 14+

deal, hence the name given to this particular variety of the game. The dealer antes as many chips as there are players to the pot and then deals each player one card face down and another face up. The former is known as the hole card. Since the remaining cards to be dealt during the hand will also be face up, it is crucial that players keep their hole cards obscured from opponents.

Play

Having examined their hidden card, each player places it face down and half covered by the face-up card. The player showing the highest face-up card, known as the 'door card', has to make the compulsory open bet. Should two or more players hold a door card of the same rank, then the opening bet is made by the player nearest to the dealer's left.

Betting follows the standard form until all bets have been equalized (see the introduction to Poker), when a second face-up card is dealt, followed by a third and then by a fourth. After each face-up card is dealt, there is another round of betting, the opening bet being made by the player showing the highest card combination, or, if there are no combinations, the highest card or cards. It is the dealer's job to confirm this by announcing, for instance, 'First King bets' or 'Pair of Sixes bets'. After the third and fourth face-ups have been dealt, the dealer should indicate which of the players still contesting the pot might be holding a possible Straight or Flush. If the cards or combinations are equal, then the player nearest to the dealer's left makes the opening bet.

Poker Hands

From highest to lowest, poker hands rank as follows:

- Five of a Kind – Four Aces and Joker (obviously this can occur only in games where wild cards are being used).
- Royal Flush – A Straight Flush up to Ace.
- Straight Flush – A combined Straight and Flush; i.e. cards in sequence and of the same suit. A hand containing Ace, Two, Three, Four and Five is the second-highest Straight or Straight Flush, ranking between Ace, King, Queen, Jack and Ten and King, Queen, Jack, Ten and Nine.
- Four of a Kind – Four cards of the same face value (known as 'Quads').
- Full House – Three of a Kind ('Trips') and a Pair. When two players hold a Full House, the highest-ranking Trips wins.
- Flush – Five cards of the same suit. If another player holds a Flush, whoever holds the highest card wins.
- Straight – A sequence of five cards in any suit; e.g. 5♦, 6♣, 7♠, 8♥, 9♣. The highest Straight is one topped by an Ace, the lowest starts with an Ace. If two players hold a Straight, the one with the highest cards wins.
- Three of a Kind – Three cards of the same face value ('Trips'); e.g. Q♠, Q♣, Q♥.
- Two Pairs – Two sets of Pairs; e.g. 3♦, 3♥ and Q♠, Q♣. Whoever holds the highest card in the two hands (the 'Kicker') wins, if two players hold matching Pairs of the same value.
- One Pair – Two cards of the same value; e.g. 3♦, 3♥ or Q♠, Q♣. If another player holds a Pair of the same value, then whoever holds the 'Kicker' wins.
- High card – A hand with no combination, but having within it the highest-ranking card among the hands in play.

Conclusion

At the end of the final betting round, each player left in the game has one card face down and four cards face up. There is now a showdown, in which players turn up their hole cards and the best hand wins. Otherwise, the game ends when all but one player have folded; that player takes the contents of the pot.

SEVEN-CARD STUD

This variant is played in much the same way as Five-Card Stud, except players receive seven cards and there are five betting rounds before the showdown.

OBJECT

To create the best-ranking hand, or bluff opponents into believing you have achieved this, in order to win the pot.

THE DEAL

Players cut the pack to decide who deals; the role of dealer then rotates on a clockwise basis. Players receive seven cards during the course of each deal, but only the five cards they select from these determine the pot's winner. The dealer antes as many chips as there are players to the pot and then deals each player two cards face down and another face up. The former are known as the hole cards. Further cards are dealt at intervals during the game, as explained in the next section.

PLAY AND CONCLUSION

The player with the lowest turn-up opens the betting. If there is a tie, the lowest card is determined by suit, the ranks, from high to low, being Spades, Hearts, Diamonds and Clubs. Each player is now dealt another turn-up. This card is called Fourth Street. A further round of betting follows, and the player whose exposed cards have the highest Poker value either bets or checks first. The alternative is to fold. The same process continues with two more face-up cards, Fifth Street and Sixth Street, being dealt, each deal being followed by another round of betting. The final card is dealt face down, so its value can be known only to the player holding it.

PLAYER A **PLAYER B** **PLAYER C**

PLAYER D

Above: In Seven-Card Stud, each player plays the best hand that he can make with the seven cards available. Player A has an Eight-high Straight, Player B has Three of a Kind, Player C an Ace-high Flush. Player D has the best hand, with a Full House.

You will need: 52 cards; Jokers optional; gambling chips/counters

Card ranking: See box on page 224

Players: Any number up to eight

Ideal for: 14+

Above: In Seven-Card Stud, players use five cards of the seven ultimately available to make a viable poker hand. Here, the player would make a Full House of Kings over Jacks, making the 2♣ and 7♦ redundant.

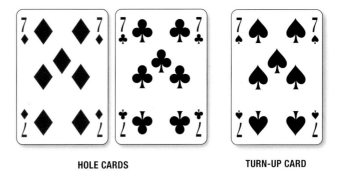

HOLE CARDS **TURN-UP CARD**

Above: Being dealt Three of a Kind after the deal, in the form of two hole cards (dealt face down) along with a face-up card, presents a huge advantage. This hand is highly likely to win the pot even if further cards do not improve on it.

A player who folds at any stage of the game must turn all of his cards face down immediately. If there is more than one player still in the game once the last betting round has been completed, all the remaining players turn up their hole cards and select five out of the seven cards as their hands. The other two cards must be discarded separately. They cannot be reclaimed. At the conclusion of each hand, known as the showdown, the highest hand wins the pot. If two hands are valued identically, the pot is split between those players.

VARIANTS

While purists prefer to play without wild cards, others argue that their inclusion adds excitement. In Seven-Card Stud, each player's lowest hole card can be wild, but only in its holder's hand. Other variations include Baseball and Football, Seven-Card Flip, and Heinz.

TEXAS HOLD 'EM

Sometimes called Hold 'em, this fast-moving high-stakes game is the game of choice across North America, where it features in many top tournaments, such as the World Series of Poker and the World Poker Tour, both held annually in Las Vegas. There are four variants of the game, which are distinguishable by their betting limits.

OBJECT

To secure the best hand, or bluff opponents into believing you have achieved this, in order to win the pot (which holds all the bets that players have made in any one deal).

THE DEAL AND PLAY

Each player receives two cards dealt face down. These are the hole or pocket cards. A first round of betting follows – this is referred to as the pre-flop – started by the player to the left of the two players who 'posted the blind'. These are the two players seated to the left of the dealer, who put a predetermined number of chips into the pot to get the game started. The player to the left of the dealer places a mandatory bet, known as the 'small blind', and the player to his left the 'big blind'. Typically, the 'big blind' is double the amount of the 'small blind'. As the deal moves clockwise around the table, each player faces the prospect of making these forced bets.

Much like most other Poker games, players can call, raise (match the previous bet and increase it) or fold. The amount players can bet varies, depending on what form of the game is being played. In fixed-limit games, this is predetermined, and the number of times each player can bet is limited to four. No limit is just what its name implies, while, in a spread-limit game, players have to bet within a specified range of amounts. In pot limit, a player can bet what is in the pot.

The Flop

After the initial betting round ends, the dealer discards the top card of the pack. This discard is called a burn card and the reason for discarding it is to prevent cheating. The dealer then flips the next three cards face up on the table. These cards are the flop. They, together with the other flop cards that are dealt later, are communal property, and can be used by any of the players to make up a winning hand.

You will need: 52-card deck, sometimes with the addition of two Jokers (some players prefer using two packs to speed up proceedings, in which case they should be of contrasting colours); gambling chips/counters

Card ranking: See box below

Players: Two to eight (experts consider five to eight is ideal)

Ideal for: 14+

POKER HANDS

From highest to lowest, poker hands rank as follows:

- Five of a Kind – Four Aces and Joker (obviously this can occur only in games where wild cards are being used).
- Royal Flush – A Straight Flush up to Ace.
- Straight Flush – A combined Straight and Flush; i.e. cards in sequence and of the same suit. A hand containing Ace, Two, Three, Four and Five is the second-highest Straight or Straight Flush, ranking between Ace, King, Queen, Jack and Ten and King, Queen, Jack, Ten and Nine.
- Four of a Kind – Four cards of the same face value (known as 'Quads').
- Full House – Three of a Kind ('Trips') and a Pair. When two players hold a Full House, the highest-ranking Trips wins.
- Flush – Five cards of the same suit. If another player holds a Flush, whoever holds the highest card wins.
- Straight – A sequence of five cards in any suit; e.g. 5♦, 6♣, 7♠, 8♥, 9♣. The highest Straight is one topped by an Ace, the lowest starts with an Ace. If two players hold a Straight, the one with the highest cards wins.
- Three of a Kind – Three cards of the same face value ('Trips'); e.g.Q♠, Q♣, Q♥.
- Two Pairs – Two sets of Pairs; e.g. 3♦, 3♥ and Q♠, Q♣. Whoever holds the highest card in the two hands (called the 'Kicker') wins, if two players hold matching Pairs of the same value.
- One Pair – Two cards of the same value; e.g. 3♦, 3♥ or Q♠, Q♣. If another player holds a Pair of the same value, then whoever holds the 'Kicker' wins.
- High card – A hand with no combination, but having within it the highest-ranking card among the hands in play.

Bluffing

At this stage of the game, there are several things to take into consideration. The first is the number of players. The more there are, the greater the chances that someone else is holding a strong hand and the more the likelihood of another player's hand fitting the flop.

As far as individual hands are concerned, the best hand to hold is a Pair of Aces, while it also helps if the cards that are held are sequential in rank. The capacity of the flop to offer potential to several players generates many opportunities to practise the art of bluffing, but knowing the right time to bluff is particularly important. A bluff works best when there are only a few players left in the game. It is always a mistake to bluff when other players are expecting it, or when it is against a dangerous flop, especially one containing an Ace. If this is the case, it is more than likely that another player will be holding a Pair of Aces.

Further Betting Rounds – the Endgame

Another round of betting follows, this time started by the player to the left of the dealer. After this, the dealer burns another card and flips a fourth card onto the table. This is the turn card. It is added to the flop. A third betting round ensues, in which the amount that can be bet doubles, after which the dealer burns a card and flips a final turn-up. This is called the river and it is also added to the flop. After this, there is a final round of betting.

CONCLUSION

All the players still in the game reveal their hands, starting with the player to the left of the last one to call. Players are allowed to use both of their hole cards and three of the cards on the table (these are the board cards); one of their hole cards and four board cards; or neither of their hole cards but all of the board cards, which is termed 'playing the board'. If the hands are tied, the player with the highest-ranking card wins. If this does not produce a result or if no one can improve on the five-card flop, the pot is divided equally between the players who are left.

Right: A pair of Aces as pocket or hole cards, sometimes referred to as 'pocket rockets', is the strongest starting hand available in Texas Hold 'em.

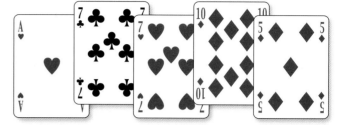

Above and right: The pair of Aces (top) matched with these five board cards makes a Full House of Aces over Sevens. However, a player may be holding a pair of Sevens, giving him Four of a Kind, which beats Full House.

PLAYER D

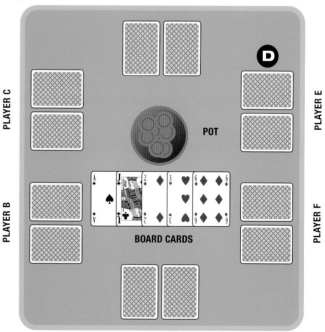

PLAYER A

Above: Recognizing the best hand available is a fundamental part of Hold 'em strategy. Here, with all five board cards revealed, after the final turn up of the river card, a player holding 4, 5 as hole cards could bet knowing that the hand was unbeatable.

Left: Australian professional poker player Joe Hecham with his US$7.5 million winnings after claiming the World Series of Poker champion title in 2005. The top 12 players competing in this tournament, which takes place annually in Las Vegas, all become millionaires.

PAI GOW POKER

This enjoyable game is a cross between the Chinese domino game Pai Gow, and Poker, which has become popular in American casinos. A single Joker is used as a wild card, and can represent an Ace or any other card to complete a Straight, Flush or Straight Flush.

OBJECT

To secure the best possible two hands from the seven cards that are dealt, which will beat those of the dealer when his turn comes to play.

THE DEAL

The dealer plays against the others on each deal. Before the deal, players each 'ante' (put in) the same stake to the pot and agree how the bank is to rotate between

---

You will need: 52 cards; one Joker; gambling chips/counters

Card ranking: See box below

Players: Two to seven

Ideal for: 14+

Left: Players are dealt seven cards in Pai Gow Poker, such as here. Each player must split their cards into two hands, one of five cards and the other of two. The five-card hand must rank higher than the two-card one. Here, the cards could be divided into 7♣, 7♦ and 2♥, 5♥, Q♠, K♦, K♠, the pair of Kings in the five-card hand ranked higher than the pair of Sevens.

POKER HANDS

From highest to lowest, poker hands rank as follows:

- Five of a Kind – Four Aces and Joker (obviously this can occur only in games where wild cards are being used).

- Royal Flush – A Straight Flush up to Ace.

- Straight Flush – A combined Straight and Flush; i.e. cards in sequence and of the same suit. A hand containing Ace, Two, Three, Four and Five is the second-highest Straight or Straight Flush, ranking between Ace, King, Queen, Jack and Ten and King, Queen, Jack, Ten and Nine.

- Four of a Kind – Four cards of the same face value (known as 'Quads').

- Full House – Three of a Kind ('Trips') and a Pair. When two players hold a Full House, the highest-ranking Trips wins.

- Flush – Five cards of the same suit. If another player holds a Flush, whoever holds the highest card wins.

- Straight – A sequence of five cards in any suit; e.g. 5♦, 6♣, 7♠, 8♥, 9♣. The highest Straight is one topped by an Ace, the lowest starts with an Ace. If two players hold a Straight, the one with the highest cards wins.

- Three of a Kind – Three cards of the same face value ('Trips'); e.g. Q♠, Q♣, Q♥.

- Two Pairs – Two sets of Pairs; e.g. 3♦, 3♥ and Q♠, Q♣. Whoever holds the highest card in the two hands (called the 'Kicker') wins, if two players hold matching Pairs of the same value.

- One Pair – Two cards of the same value; e.g. 3♦, 3♥ or Q♠, Q♣. If another player holds a Pair of the same value, then whoever holds the 'Kicker' wins.

- High card – A hand with no combination, but having within it the highest-ranking card among the hands in play.

---

them. Each player should be given the chance to deal the same number of times during a session. The players are each then dealt seven cards face down, which the players have to split into two hands, one of two cards and the other of five cards.

The five-card hand must rank higher than the two-card one. If, for instance, the two-card hand was a Pair of Aces, then the corresponding five-card hand must be two Pairs or better. The Joker may replace an Ace or whatever card is needed to complete a Straight, a Flush or a Straight Flush, but nothing else. At this stage of the game, the dealer's cards remain untouched.

PLAY

Players place their two hands face down, after which the dealer's seven cards are turned up and formed into two hands. All the players then expose their cards.

CONCLUSION

The winner and loser are determined by comparing the player's and dealer's hands. If a player wins both of these hands, the dealer pays out the amount staked by that player, and vice versa if the dealer's hands are better.

If the dealer wins one hand, but a player wins the other, it is deemed a 'push' and no stakes change hands. If either hand is tied, the dealer wins the hand.

FREAK-HAND POKER

This form of Poker is aptly named, since, as well as the standard hands, it features others made up of unorthodox card combinations. Freak hands were originally devised to liven up games like Draw Poker, where, without them, the majority of hands were won on Two Pairs. Their use is now mostly confined to Lowball Poker.

Freak hands first made their appearance towards the end of the 19th century, when the Blaze – a five-card hand containing five picture cards other than Four of a Kind – became widely recognized, along with the Blaze Full, a Full House in picture cards.

Above: A hand of five picture cards is a Blaze. It often ranks below Four of a Kind, but above a Full House.

Above: A Full House composed of picture cards is known as a Blaze Full.

Other examples include a Dutch Straight (Alternate Straight) – which is a sequence of every other card, such as Two, Four, Six, Eight and Ten – Kilters and Skeets. A Kilter is a hand starting with an Ace, followed by cards of alternate value down to Nine, and a Skeet contains a Two, Five, Nine, either a Three or a Four, and a Six, Seven or Eight. The Eight is the Skeet. A Skeet Flush is when all the cards are of the same suit.

A Big Dog consists of cards ranking from Ace down to Nine with no Pair, while a Little Dog, which often ranks below it but above a Straight, consists of a Two to a Seven.

Above: A Little Dog, which can rank above a Straight.

Above: A Big Dog, which always ranks above Little Dog.

Above: A Little Tiger, which can rank above a Big Dog.

Above: A Big Tiger, which often ranks just below a Flush.

Little Tiger is a hand consisting of cards from Three up to Nine with no Pair, while Big Tiger is Eight to King. It ranks just below a Flush. A Bobtail Flush consists of four cards of the same suit and a Bobtail Straight one of four cards in consecutive order, both of which are open ended. A Flush House consists of three cards of one suit and two of another. The ranking of these combinations is often based on which of these hands are included in the game.

Above: A Bobtail Flush.

Above: A Bobtail Straight.

Left: A Flush House can rank between a Bobtail Straight and Bobtail Flush.

FREAK DRAWS

As well as freak hands, Poker also sometimes features freak draws, although these are down to luck and usually greatly defy probability. In Lowball, drawing three cards and making a Six or better is a freak draw.

In Draw Poker, if a player draws three cards to two cards of the same suit to make a Flush, this, too, is regarded as a freak. The phenomenon is sometimes called a Gardena miracle, after the city of Gardena, in southern California, which was once the poker-playing capital of the USA.

DEALER'S CHOICE GAMES

In Poker, dealer's choice means exactly what it says. The player dealing selects the game to be played on his particular deal, as opposed to playing one game exclusively for the entire playing session. In friendly games, the choice can be pretty well unlimited, but casinos usually restrict it to a small number of possibilities. Some, like Fifty-Two and Forty-Two, are variants of Draw Poker, where four or five cards are dealt face down, while others, such as Razz and Chicago, are played in the same way as Seven-Card Stud, where cards are dealt, face up and face down, at intervals throughout the game.

DRAW GAMES

FIFTY-TWO

Each player is dealt five face-down cards, known as hole cards, with two more cards being placed face down on the table. After a round of betting, one of these cards is turned face up, followed by the other one after a second betting round. Players may draw up to three cards, but, to make their hands, they must use all their hole cards, or three hole cards and both board cards (the exposed cards dealt to the table). A combination of four hole cards and a single board card is against the rules. It is not recommended for more than seven players since they will often run out of cards.

FORTY-TWO

The key differences between this game and Fifty-Two are that only four hole cards are dealt, players may draw only up to two cards and any five cards can be used to make up their hands. Note that in both games, the dealer enjoys a significant advantage, since he knows how many cards other players have drawn before having to make a draw.

STUD GAMES

RAZZ AND CHICAGO

In high-card Poker, the highest hand wins; in low-card Poker, the lowest one. Razz is played for low only. Chicago, on the other hand, can be played either high or low. In High Chicago, the holder of the highest Spade as a hole (face-down) card splits the pot with the holder of the highest hand. In Low Chicago, the player holding the lowest Spade splits the pot. If no player has a Spade as a hole card, the highest hand wins the pot outright.

NO PEEK STUD

Here, each player is dealt seven cards, but no player is allowed to look at them. Instead, the cards must be placed face down in a pile. The player to the dealer's left turns over a card, after which there is a round of betting. The next player then turns over cards until he has the higher hand. Another betting round follows. The process continues round the table until all the players run out of cards, when the pot goes to the highest hand.

Below: Playing High Chicago, Player A has a seemingly stronger hand, with a Full House of Queens over Jacks, but Player B has the A♠ as a hole card, which means that he can claim half the pot.

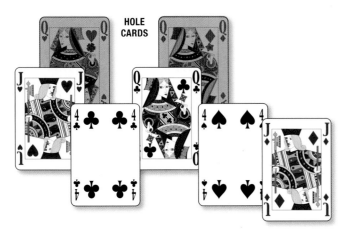

PLAYER A'S HAND

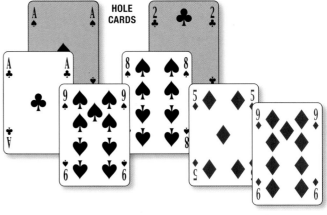

PLAYER B'S HAND

POKER HANDS

From highest to lowest, poker hands rank as follows:

- Five of a Kind – Four Aces and Joker (obviously this can occur only in games where wild cards are being used).

- Royal Flush – A Straight Flush up to Ace.

- Straight Flush – A combined Straight and Flush; i.e. cards in sequence and of the same suit. A hand containing Ace, Two, Three, Four and Five is the second-highest Straight or Straight Flush, ranking between Ace, King, Queen, Jack and Ten and King, Queen, Jack, Ten and Nine.

- Four of a Kind – Four cards of the same face value (known as 'Quads').

- Full House – Three of a Kind ('Trips') and a Pair. When two players hold a Full House, the highest-ranking Trips wins.

- Flush – Five cards of the same suit. If another player holds a Flush, whoever holds the highest card wins.

- Straight – A sequence of five cards in any suit; e.g. 5♦, 6♣, 7♠, 8♥, 9♣. The highest Straight is one topped by an Ace, the lowest starts with an Ace. If two players hold a Straight, the one with the highest cards wins.

- Three of a Kind – Three cards of the same face value ('Trips'); e.g. Q♠, Q♣, Q♥.

- Two Pairs – Two sets of Pairs; e.g. 3♦, 3♥ and Q♠, Q♣. Whoever holds the highest card in the two hands (called the 'Kicker') wins, if two players hold matching Pairs of the same value.

- One Pair – Two cards of the same value; e.g. 3♦, 3♥ or Q♠, Q♣. If another player holds a Pair of the same value, then whoever holds the 'Kicker' wins.

- High card – A hand with no combination, but having within it the highest-ranking card among the hands in play.

FOLLOW THE QUEEN

Each player starts with two face-down hole cards, followed by a face-up card. In this game, a player with a Queen in his hand (either turned up or face down) treats the Queen as a wild card. If a Queen is dealt as a turn-up, the next turn-up dealt is a wild card, as are the other three cards of the same rank. The process is repeated each time a Queen is turned up, the previous wild card reverting to its original status. The best hand wins.

Left: A feature of most Lowball games is the fact that Straights and Flushes are not counted. In Razz, the lowest hand is a 'wheel', a Straight of 5, 4, 3, 2, A.

THREE CARDS OR FEWER

THREE-CARD DROP

In Three-Card Drop, each player is dealt three cards face down. Players make an initial ante to the pot. Other than this, there is no betting, nor is there a draw, while there are also no common cards. (A common card is a card dealt face up to be used by all players at the showdown, when the highest hand wins the pot.) After examining their cards, players decide whether to drop out of or stay in the game. If the decision is to stay in, the player concerned takes a chip and places it in his hand. A player who wishes to 'drop', that is, not take part, indicates this by not taking a chip.

If all players drop, there is no winner. They ante again and the game is replayed. If more than one player stays in, there is a showdown. This, however, does not end the game. All the losing players must fund a new pot by putting in an equal number of chips to those in the pot that has just been won, and re-ante. After this, a new hand is dealt. The process goes on until only one player declares himself to be in, at which point he wins the final pot and the game ends.

GUTS

In Guts, players are dealt only two cards and must announce if they are in or out simultaneously. A player may unclench a fist to reveal a chip if he is in, or players may all hold their cards just above the table, dropping them to indicate a fold. Those players still in now reveal their cards. The highest Pair wins – or the highest card if there are no Pairs. The winner takes the pot, the losers staking the amount it contained to form a new one ready for the next deal. Play goes on until only one player is willing to continue. He takes the final pot. If no one is prepared to play, the players keep going with the same cards until someone is prepared to bet. Otherwise, the hands are revealed and the player who would have won is penalized by having to match the contents of the pot.

Left: In Follow the Queen, whenever a Queen is turned up, the next turn-up to be dealt is a wild card, as are the other three cards of the same rank.

BRAG

Thought to be derived from a Tudor card game called Primero, which was popular in the days of Elizabeth I, Brag has a long and illustrious history. While it is similar to Poker, the way in which bets are made is different. In the classic game, hands consist of three cards and the highest hand is a Prial (Three of a Kind) of Threes. There are several varieties, but all are what are termed hard-score games – that is, those played for gambling chips or cash.

OBJECT

To finish with the best-ranked hand and scoop the pot.

ANTES

Before play begins, players should agree on several points: the initial stake, or ante, to be put into the pot before each deal; the maximum and minimum initial bet and amount by which bets can be raised; and any variations to the basic rules such as whether or not wild cards are to be played.

You will need: 52 cards; gambling chips/counters
Card ranking: Standard (except for wild cards – see below)
Players: Four to eight is optimal
Ideal for: 14+

BRAG HANDS

From highest to lowest, Brag hands rank as follows:

- Prial – A set of three cards of equal rank (a set of Threes is the best possible Prial, followed by a set of Aces down to Twos, the lowest).
- Running Flush – Three cards of the same suit (highest is an Ace, Two, Three).
- Run – Three consecutive cards of mixed suits (highest is an Ace, Two, Three).
- Flush – Three non-consecutive cards of the same suit.
- Pair – Two cards of equal rank.
- High Card – A hand consisting of three cards that do not fit into any of the above combinations. It ranks according to the highest card in it. There is no ranking of suits.

WILD CARDS

In Brag, wild cards are known as floaters – they were once called braggers or turners. Either all Twos can be wild, or just the black ones. The One-Eyed Jacks, the J♠ and the J♥ (so called because only one eye shows), can also be wild – so can the K♥, known as the Suicide King because the sword the King carries appears to pass through his head.

A Joker or Jokers can be added to the pack to serve as extra wild cards. Such cards can replace any natural card in the pack. If, however, two hands are equal, a hand with no wild cards always beats one with wild cards in it, while a hand with fewer wild cards beats one with more of them. Thus, a hand of three Fives will beat a hand of two Sixes and a wild card, or a Seven and two wild cards.

THE DEAL

The cards are shuffled only for the first deal. In subsequent ones, this happens only if the previous deal was won by a Prial. Otherwise, the cards are simply added to the bottom of the pack as players fold. Each player receives three cards dealt singly face down to the table. However, each player is obliged to contribute one chip into the pot before any cards are dealt.

Above: The cards are ranked by suit in the conventional order of ♠♥♦♣, which means a Spade will beat a Heart of the same rank and a Diamond will beat a Club. This is only needed when two players have the same hands but in different suit combinations (as shown). In this case, the combination at the top wins, due to the Ace being a Spade.

PRIAL   PRIAL   PRIAL

Left: A Prial of Threes is the highest possible hand, and a Prial of Twos is the least strong Prial possible. The second of the three hands, although ostensibly a Prial of Threes, would be beaten by a hand with no wild cards.

RUNNING FLUSH   RUN   FLUSH

Left: Examples of a Running Flush, Run and Flush. After a Prial, these are, in descending order, the next highest hands in Brag.

PLAY AND BETTING

Once dealt, cards may either be examined or left as they are should their holder take the option of playing blind. If a player decides to do this, he takes part in the betting in the normal way, but any bets are worth double.

At any stage, when it is that player's turn to bet, he can decide to look at the cards before making the decision of whether to bet or to fold. In that case, he ceases to be a blind player.

The player to the left of the dealer has the chance to bet first. The options are to bet any amount between the minimum and maximum stakes that have been previously agreed, or to fold.

A player who runs out of chips during the betting, but who still wants to stay in the game, may 'cover the kitty' by placing his hand over the pot. The other players then start a new pot and continue playing.

The process continues until there are only two players left in the game. They carry on betting until one drops out, in which case the surviving player wins the pot without having to show his hand. The alternative is for either to 'see' the other by doubling the previous player's bet. Both players then expose their hands, the one who called for the showdown exposing his hand first.

VARIANTS

In Five-Card Brag, each player receives five cards, discarding two face down before play starts. In Seven-Card Brag, anyone dealt Four of a Kind wins the pot automatically and there is a new deal. Otherwise, each player discards a card and forms the others into two hands, placing the higher one to the left and the lower one to the right. The higher hand is played first. The procedure is the same in Nine-Card Brag; each player ends up with three hands, ordered and played from highest to lowest.

CONCLUSION

The player with the highest hand wins the pot. If the two hands are equal, the player who paid to 'see', loses. If a player has covered the kitty, his hand is compared at the end of play to the hand of the 'winner', and the better of the two hands wins it. If one player is playing open and the other blind, the rules state that 'you cannot see a blind man'. The only options are to continue to bet or to fold. If both players are blind, betting twice the blind stake forces the hands to be compared.

MUS

A game from the Basque part of Spain, Mus is unusual: although its mechanics resemble those of Poker in that cards are drawn and each player then bets on his hand, it is played up to a fixed total of points. And unlike Poker, players are allowed to signal to their partners which cards they hold. Suits are irrelevant. What matters are the cards' ranks and values. In Mus, originally played with a 40-card Spanish pack, Threes count as Kings and Twos as Aces. The cards also have point values – a *Rey* (King), *Caballo* (Horseman) and *Sota* (Ten) are each worth 10 points, while the other cards score at face value. This becomes important in the final betting round of each deal.

OBJECT

To score points through various card combinations. The game is not usually played for money.

THE DEAL

The player to the dealer's right, known as the *Mano*, is the person who leads play, and all procedures pass to the right. All players are dealt four cards singly and the remaining cards are stacked face down to form the stock. Players can call '*Mus*' if they want to try to improve their hands by discarding, or can say '*No hay mus*' if happy with the cards as dealt. All four players must agree to the exchange, otherwise none can be made.

The players must then all discard from one to four cards, which are replaced by cards from the top of the stock. The process can be repeated until a player calls a halt to it. If the stock is exhausted before this, a new stock is formed from the shuffled discards.

You will need: 40-card Spanish pack; 22 stones or counters
Card rankings: *Rey* (King), *Caballo* (Horseman), *Sota* (Ten), and then Seven down to Ace
Players: Four players in partnerships of two
Ideal for: 14+

PLAY AND BETTING

There are four rounds of betting, each for a particular combination of cards, carried out in strict order (see box below). In each round of betting, the *Mano* starts by deciding to pass or to bet. If the former, the next player to the right takes over. If no one bets, the *Mano* starts the next betting round.

If someone bets in the *Grande* and *Chica* betting rounds, the opposing players can fold, match the bet, or raise it. This is when signalling between partners becomes important. Closing the eyes means poor cards,

MUS HANDS

There are four valid card combinations: *Grande*, *Chica*, *Pares* and *Juego*, on which players bet in strict order. They comprise the following:

- *Grande* – a bet that one or the other player in a partnership holds the highest hand.

- *Chica* – a bet that one or the other player in a partnership holds the lowest hand.

- *Pares* – a bet for the best-paired hand, a hand where two or more cards rank equally. Sub-rankings within *Pares* are:
  a. *Par Simple* (the lowest), two cards of equal rank.
  b. *Medias*, three cards of the same rank and one of a different one.
  c. *Dobles* (the highest), two pairs.

If no betting takes place, a *Par Simple* is worth one point, a *Medias* two and a *Dobles* three.

- *Juego* – a declaration that the cards in hand are worth at least 31 points. If no player can declare *Juego*, the alternative is *Punto*, denoting a hand worth 30 points or less.

Above: Mus was originally played with a 40-card Spanish pack, organized into four suits, the Aces of which are shown clockwise from the top: *Bastos* (Clubs), *Copas* (Cups), *Espadas* (Swords) and *Oros* (Golds or Coins). The three distinctive court or face cards in each suit are the *Rey* (King), *Caballo* (Horseman) and *Sota* (Ten).

Left: Three examples of *Pares:* a *Par Simple* (the lowest, being two cards of equal rank); a *Medias* (being three cards of the same rank and one of a different one); and *Dobles* (the highest, being two pairs).

Below: After the last betting round, players lay down their hands. Player A has a *Par Simple* as does Player C. Player D has *Medias* (Three of a Kind), but Player B wins with *Dobles* (two pairs).

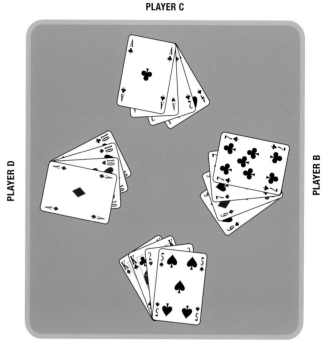

PLAYER C

PLAYER D

PLAYER B

PLAYER A

for instance, a hand of Four, Five, Six and Seven. In some versions, a player with these cards can expose them immediately and be dealt a replacement hand, provided that the declaration is made before calling "*Mus*".

Biting the lower lip means three Kings. Pouting the lips means that the player concerned would like to exchange some cards or it can mean that the player is holding three Kings and an Ace. Inclining the head to the right means that the player would prefer not to change cards. Shrugging the shoulder means that a player has a *Punto* of 30, while sticking out the tip of one's tongue means that the player is holding three Aces.

Betting continues until one side or the other folds, or sees the last raise. In the latter case, there is a showdown. Before any bets can be made in the *Pares* and *Juego* stages, each player must say if he actually holds the requisite cards. If at least one player from each partnership says 'Yes', a round of betting follows. If both players in one partnership say 'No', but either or both members of the opposing one say 'Yes', they can score the basic number of points for what they hold, but betting is disallowed. If all four players say 'No', there is no score. Instead, players then bet on who has the best *Punto*, that is, a hand worth 30 or fewer points

One final bet, an *Órdago*, is a call for an immediate showdown. The opposing players must either fold or see the bet. The outcome of the entire game is determined by who holds the best hand for that particular round.

SCORING

After the last betting round, players all show their cards, and the hand is scored round by round, although only for points that have not as yet been claimed and taken. These are represented by tokens called *piedras* (stones), 22 of which are placed in a saucer in the centre of the table. A minimum bet is two stones.

In each partnership, one player is responsible for collecting the stones. For every five stones won, four are returned to the saucer and one passed to the other partner. Each of these is worth five points.

When the player in charge of the *piedras* has collected seven such stones, he must call 'Dentro' ('inside') to alert the opposing players to the fact that the team is within five points of winning the game.

CONCLUSION

A match is three games, the side winning two of them winning the contest.

PRIMERO

This intriguing game, which is still played in parts of central Italy as Goffo, or Bambara, originated in Renaissance times. It is thought likely that a variant of it was favoured by Henry VIII of England. It has strong similarities to many aspects of modern-day Poker, although it is based on four-card, rather than five-card, combinations.

OBJECT
To score points through various card combinations and to finish with the highest-scoring hand.

THE DEAL
Before the deal, players each ante an agreed amount to the pot. The ante is the stake that each player must put into the pool before receiving a hand or new cards. Each player is dealt four cards, two at a time. The turn to deal and bet passes to the left.

PLAY AND BETTING
Any player dealt a winning hand can call for an immediate showdown, in which the best hand wins the pot. If no one wins outright, each player makes the necessary discards and is dealt replacements. There may be a further round of betting at this stage.

Otherwise, play starts with the player to the dealer's left, each player in turn having the choice of three options: to stake, bid or pass. In order to bid, the previous bet must be staked, that is, matched, before the new bid can be announced. Any bid must specify a points total, the type of hand and the amount being bid. The hand type must be higher than the one bid by the previous bidder, or the points total must be higher than the

You will need: 40-card deck (standard pack with Eights to Tens removed); gambling chips/counters

Card ranking: King, Queen, Jack, Seven down to Two, and Ace

Players: Four to eight

Ideal for: 14+

preceding one. A player who passes must discard one or two cards and draw replacements. Unlike Poker, it is impossible simply to fold.

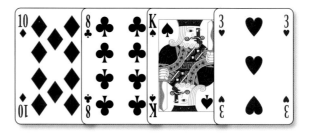

Above: A *Primero*, which is the lowest-ranking hand in the game, consists of one card in each suit.

SCORING
Ties are broken in favour of the hand with the highest point count. For this purpose, each rank scores a specific number of points. The court cards are worth 10 points each, and Aces 16. Sixes and Sevens count as three times their face value. Hence, a Six counts as 18 and a Seven as 21. Twos to Fives are worth 10 points plus their face value. Thus, a Four is worth 14 points and a Five 15.

Above: A Fifty-Five, the second-lowest-ranking hand in the game.

Above: Four of a Kind (Chorus), the highest-ranking hand in the game.

PRIMERO HANDS
There are four possible winning hands, which are detailed below from highest to lowest. Hand ranking wins over the highest score unless in a tie.

- Chorus – Four of a kind.
- Flush (or *Fluxus*) – A hand in which all four cards are of the same suit.
- Fifty-Five (or *Maximus*) – A hand consisting of Ace, Six and Seven of one suit plus one other card.
- *Primero* – A hand consisting of one card of each suit.

CONCLUSION
The game continues until a win is claimed. If there is a tie, the hand with the highest points wins.

POCH

This game is at least 500 years old. It has spread from its German homeland as far as North America, where variants of it are played under the names of Tripoli and Three in One. To play, you need a special board called a *Pochbrett*, which has nine compartments, each of which holds the chips bet on specific winning cards and combinations.

OBJECT

To be the first player to get rid of all his cards.

THE DEAL

Before the deal, players dress the *Pochbrett* board, each putting one chip into each of its nine compartments – Ace, King, Queen, Jack, Ten, Marriage, Sequence, Poch (marked with a Joker on the board) and the unlabelled centre pot. From the 32-card deck, players are dealt five cards each, the next one being turned face up to determine the 'pay suit'. If a ready-made board is not to hand, it is fairly easy to make your own using paper.

Left: A *Pochbrett* board has nine sections for holding gambling chips, which are bet on specific winning cards and combinations.

PLAY AND SCORING

In the game's first stage, holding the Ace, King, Queen and Jack of the pay suit means winning the chips in the matching compartment. Holding the King and Queen wins the Marriage compartment, while holding Seven, Eight and Nine of the pay suit wins the Sequence compartment; if no one declares these, or if an Ace, King, Queen, Jack or Ten is turned up as the pay suit card, the chips are carried forward.

You will need: Standard deck with Twos to Sixes removed; gambling chips/counters; (drawing of a) Pochbrett board

Card ranking: Ace down to Seven

Players: Three to six

Ideal for: 14+

Left: A copy of a cover of a Poch boardgame (*c.*1897), with a picture of the Joker. It is currently on display at the Munich Municipal Museum.

In the second stage, players bet on who has the best combinations of cards. Any set of Four of a Kind beats any set of Three of a Kind, and any set of Three of a Kind beats any Pair. A set of higher-ranking cards always beats the same number of lower-ranking ones. If two players hold Pairs of the same rank, one containing a card from the pay suit is better. Four Eights, for instance, beats three Kings, which beats two Nines, which beats the Queens of Hearts and Diamonds, which beats the Queens of Spades and Clubs, if Diamonds or Hearts is the pay suit.

Players bet by stating '*Ich poche*' and how many chips they are betting. The alternative is to pass. After the initial bet, players can either match it, raise or fold. The winner takes all the chips that were bet, plus the chips in the Poch compartment.

The previous stage's winner starts the final one by placing a card face up on top of the centre compartment on the board. Whoever holds the next higher card of the same suit then plays it, the process continuing until no one can play the next card required. The player of the last card of that sequence starts play again.

CONCLUSION

The first player to get rid of all his cards wins, taking the contents of the centre compartment. Other players forfeit a chip for each card they hold in hand.

BOUILLOTTE

This game was invented at the time of the French Revolution as the official replacement for a game called Brelan, which the Revolutionary government decided to ban. It was popular in France until the late 19th and early 20th centuries, when it was slowly but surely supplanted in French affections by the newly fashionable game of Poker.

OBJECT

To finish with the highest-ranking combination or suit, and so win the pot and/or bonus chips.

STRADDLING

Each player starts with a stack of 30 chips, known as the *cave* (stack). Players ante a chip to the pot, the dealer adding an extra chip. The ante is the stake that each player must put into the pool before receiving a hand or new cards. The player to the dealer's right can now elect to double the size of the pot. This is known as a straddle. The next player can do the same and so on round to the dealer. If a player chooses not to straddle, or does not have enough chips to do so, the straddling ends and the cards are dealt.

THE DEAL

Each player receives three cards, the dealer turning the next card face up to establish the trump suit.

PLAY

Players bet on who has the best hand, the first to bet being the player to the right of the last player to straddle. He can either open or pass. To open, a player must bet at least as many chips as the highest previous stake. The others may call (match) the bet, raise it or fold.

SCORING

Bonus chips from each of the opposing players are given to the holder of a *Brelan Carré* or *Brelan* (see box). If no one holds a *Brelan Carré* or a *Brelan*, the points for the cards held by all the players, including those who folded, are calculated suit by suit. Aces score 11 points, Kings and Queens 10 points each and the others score at face value. The suit with the highest total is the winning suit and the player holding the highest card of that suit wins the pot.

You will need: 20 cards comprising Aces, Kings, Queens, Nines and Eights; gambling chips/counters

Card ranking: Ace highest, Eight lowest

Players: Four

Ideal for: 10+

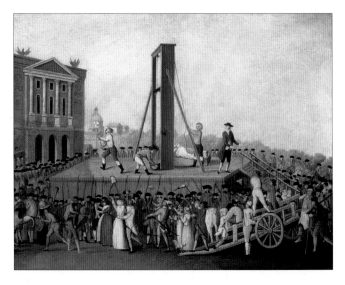

Above: Bouillotte was invented during the years of the French Revolution.

BOUILLOTTE HANDS

From highest to lowest, Bouillotte hands rank as follows:

- *Brelan Carré* – Three of a Kind of the same rank as the turn-up. It is worth a bonus three chips.
- *Brelan* – Three of a Kind. It is worth one extra chip. If more than one player holds a *Brelan*, the highest wins.

Right: Three of a Kind (*Brelan*). In the event of a tie, the best hand is one that matches the rank of the turn-up, making a *Brelan Carré*. If neither matches, the highest-ranked *Brelan* wins.

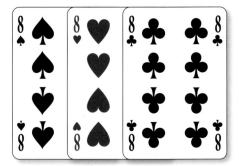

CONCLUSION

Betting continues until there are only two players left, when the first to call a bet forces a showdown.

SEVEN TWENTY-SEVEN

In this American vying game, the court cards are worth half a point each and number cards their face values. Aces can count for either a point or 11 points, depending on whether they are being played low, high – or, indeed, both.

You will need: 52 cards; gambling chips/counters

Card ranking: Ace high or low, remaining cards Kings down to Twos

Players: Four to ten

Ideal for: 10+

OBJECT

To end up with a hand that is as near to seven or 27 points as possible.

THE DEAL

Players ante their initial stakes to the pot. The ante is the stake that each player must put into the pot before receiving a hand or new cards. After this, one card is dealt face up to each player and another one face

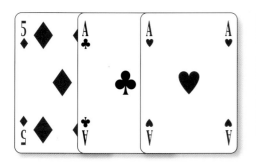

Left: The perfect hand in Seven Twenty-Seven: two Aces and a Five, the cards adding up to seven for Aces low and 27 for Aces high.

PLAYER C

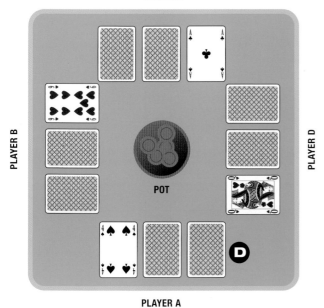

POT

PLAYER B

PLAYER D

PLAYER A

Above: Once players have examined the face-up and face-down cards they have been dealt, each player, starting with the one to the dealer's left, may ask for an extra face-down card.

down. Once the face-down cards have been examined, each player, starting with the one to the dealer's left, may ask for an extra face-down card to be dealt.

PLAY AND BETTING

The first round of betting follows, initiated by the player to the dealer's left, who may either pass or bet any amount within the agreed maximum and minimum betting limits. If he passes, the chance to open the betting passes to the next player and so on round the table.

Following this, the other players can fold, or call (match) or raise the bet. If all the players but one fold, that player takes all the bets, the cards are thrown in and the next in turn deals. Otherwise, betting continues until the stakes are equalized – this happens, when, after one player has bet or raised, all the other players call or fold.

After each betting round, the remaining players can each ask for an extra card to be dealt to them face down. The alternative is to play the hand as it is. Another betting round follows.

SCORING AND CONCLUSION

When no player asks for an extra card, there is a showdown. Everyone still in the game reveals his cards. There are two winners – the players whose totals are nearest to seven and 27, respectively. They split the pot equally. In the event of a tie, players split the relevant part of the pot. For example, if two players score 6 points and one scores 24, the player with 24 takes half the pot and the players with 6 take one quarter of the pot each. If no one has scored exactly seven or 27 (the perfect hand to do this is Five, Ace and Ace), the nearest wins.

To win, you have to be below or equal to the target. This means that you cannot win the seven pot if your score is more than seven, or anything at all if your score is over 27. Under beats over means that, if the differences are equal, it is better to be under the target, not over it. For example, if the four players have scored 5.5, 7.5, 26 and 28 respectively, the ones with 5.5 and 26 win.

10 | QUASI-TRUMP GAMES

BRITISH CARD GAME AUTHORITY DAVID PARLETT COINED THIS PHRASE FOR A STRANGE GROUP OF TRICK-TAKING GAMES, EACH WITH ITS OWN IDIOSYNCRASIES. PLAYERS NEED NOT FOLLOW SUIT AND INSTEAD CAN PLAY ANY CARD THEY LIKE. THERE IS NO CONVENTIONAL TRUMP SUIT — CERTAIN CARDS, OFTEN WITH SPECIAL NAMES, ACT AS QUASI-TRUMPS OR HAVE SPECIAL POWERS OF THEIR OWN. THIS APPLIES TO SEVENS, WHICH ALWAYS WIN THE TRICK, BUT ONLY WHEN LED.

Until Charles Cotton published *The Complete Gamester* in 1674, rules of card games were rarely written down and, when they were, they were almost always never complete. Generally speaking, they seem to have been transmitted orally. The French comic genius François Rabelais (*c.*1483–1553) noted the names of games, but these were not standardized and varied from place to place. Given all the variations, it is surprising that so many games managed to survive.

It is now accepted that the first trick-taking games probably first appeared in around 1400. Karnöffel is among the first, with reference to it dating back to 1426. Its rules were thought to be totally lost until it was discovered that a game called Kaiserspiel, which fitted Karnöffel's general description almost exactly, was still being played in a few places south of Lucerne in Switzerland. Judging by researchers' reconstructions, Karnöffel was an anarchic affair. Any card could be played to a trick, players could talk freely about the cards in their hand and what they wanted their partners to do. Also, only some of the cards in the suit designated as trumps had trick-taking powers: namely, the Jack, the Seven (if led), the Six and the Two. When it was introduced, Catholics were outraged that the Pope, as one trump is named, was outranked by the Devil, while royalty were not amused to see Kings being beaten by low cards.

Above: Charles Cotton, 17th-century author of *The Complete Gamester*, was one of the first to write down the rules of several quasi-trump games.

WATTEN

This eccentric game originated in Bavaria, from where it spread to the Tyrol. It started life as a four-player partnership game, but there are versions for two and three players. In Bavaria, it is played with a 32-card German-suited pack; the Tyrolean version introduces the 6♦ as an extra wild card.

OBJECT

To score two or more game points by taking three tricks, or for one partnership to bluff the other into conceding.

TRUMPS AND RANKING

Watten is distinguished in having three permanent top trumps, the K♥, the 7♦ and the 7♣. Individually, these are known as *Maxi*, *Belli* and *Spritzer* and collectively as *Kritischen*. There is also a separate *Schlag* (trump rank) and trump suit. The cards of the trump rank are called *Schläge* (strikers), the highest being the *Hauptschlag* (chief striker) – the card that also belongs to the trump suit. The three other strikers rank immediately below it, followed by the remaining cards of the trump suit. The player to the dealer's left selects the trump rank and the dealer names the trump suit.

You will need: Standard pack with Sixes and below removed

Card ranking: Non-trump ranking is Ace down to Seven; for trump ranking, see below

Players: Four, in partnerships of two

Ideal for: 14+

THE DEAL AND PLAY

The dealer shuffles the 32 cards, which are then cut by the player to the right. If the cut card is a top trump, the cutter may take it. If the next one is the second-top trump, the dealer may take that and, if the next card is the third, the cutter can take it again. Each player is dealt five cards in packets of three and two, although the dealer and cutter get fewer if they have added to their hands.

After the deal, the trump rank and suit are announced, and the player to the dealer's left leads to the trick. If the chief striker is led, then a top trump, another striker or suit trump must be played if possible. Otherwise, there is no obligation to follow suit.

Left: There are three permanent top trumps: the K♥, 7♦ and 7♣, collectively called *Kritischen*.

SCORING

The score can be affected by any prior betting, which can take place at any time after the announcement of trump rank and suit by a player saying 'Gehen' (go). If the opposing side respond with 'Schauen' (see), the stakes are raised to three game points, or they can concede. Betting can continue indefinitely, although a team with nine or 10 game points is *Gespannt* (tight) and not allowed to bet further. Game is either 11 or 15 points.

PLAYER C

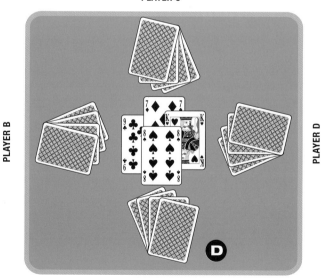

PLAYER B

PLAYER D

PLAYER A

Above: In this hand of Watten, Player B has announced Nine as the trump rank, and the dealer has announced Clubs as the trump suit. Player B leads the *Hauptschlag* (chief striker – the card belonging to both the trump suit and the trump rank), forcing the next player to lay a top trump, another striker or a card from the trump suit. Player C lays the 7♦ (*Belli*), but Player D tops this with the K♥ (*Maxi*). Player A discards, allowing Player D to take the trick.

CONCLUSION

Hands continue until three tricks are taken (if there is no betting, the team taking them scores two points) or a partnership is bluffed into conceding.

KARNÖFFEL

Claimed to be the oldest trick-taking game in the Western world, Karnöffel was one of the first to have a trump suit, properly termed the 'chosen' suit. This reconstruction is based on the research of US card authority Glenn Overby.

You will need:	Standard pack with Aces removed
Card reading:	King down to Two, except in trumps (see below)
Players:	Four, in partnerships of two
Ideal for:	14+

OBJECT

To take the most tricks out of five to win a hand. Players agree how many hands make up a game at the start.

TRUMP SUIT RANKINGS

The trump suit ranks differently, and certain cards have trick-taking powers. The Jack of trumps (*Karnöffel*) ranks highest, beating all other cards. The Seven of trumps, the Devil, comes second, but enjoys that status only if it is led. Following this is the Six of trumps (the Pope) and the Two of trumps (*Kaiser*), then the Three of trumps (the *Oberstecher*) and the Four of trumps (the *Unterstecher*). These last two cannot beat any of the above trumps. The Three of trumps cannot beat a King, and the Four of trumps cannot beat a Queen or King. A Five of trumps, the *Farbenstecher*, cannot beat any of the court cards or any of the above trumps.

THE DEAL

Each player receives five cards dealt singly, the first face up, the others face down. The lowest-ranking face-up card determines which suit is trumps. In the event of a tie, trumps are set by the first card of that rank to be dealt.

PLAY

The player to the dealer's left leads to the first trick. The person who plays the highest card of the suit led or the highest trump wins the trick and leads to the next. Subsequently, any card can be played, since there is no requirement to follow suit. During the course of play, players are allowed to communicate freely with one another. In fact, most of the important cards have signals linked to them. It is even legal to signal cards that are not held in order to try to confuse the opposition.

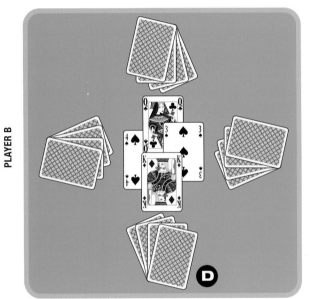

Above: Here, Spades are trumps. Player B leads the 4♠ (*Unterstecher*) but this is not strong enough to beat the Queen played by Player C. Player D plays the 3♠ (*Oberstecher*), winning the trick until Player A tops it with a King.

CONCLUSION

The partnership taking the most tricks out of the five available wins the hand. The player who led to the first trick then deals the next hand. Partnerships agree at the start how many hands will make up a game.

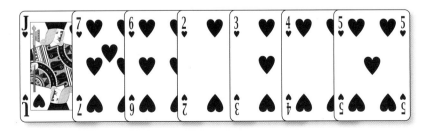

Left: Trumps (here assumed to be Hearts) have special ranks and trick-taking powers. The Jack (*Karnöffel*) ranks highest, followed by the Seven (the Devil), but only if this is led to a trick. Next comes the Six (the Pope), the Two (*Kaiser*), the Three (*Oberstecher*), the Four (*Unterstecher*) and the Five (*Farbenstecher*).

BRUS

A Swedish partnership game, Brus is unique because it is played with a mixture of 18 playable and 14 unplayable cards.

You will need: Standard pack with Fives and below removed

Card ranking: See 'Playable and Unplayable Cards'

Players: Four or six, playing in partnerships of two or three

Ideal for: 14+

OBJECT

To score six strokes (game points) over as many deals as it takes. In each deal, a game point is won by the partnership that wins six tricks.

PLAYABLE AND UNPLAYABLE CARDS

Playable cards are the only ones that can be played to tricks, while the unplayable ones are unusable, the exception being the K♣, which can score if a side that has taken five tricks holds it. For this reason, it is known as the 'outcome card'.

From highest to lowest, all playable cards are the J♣ (*Spit*), the 8♠ (*Dull*) and the K♥ (*Brus*). These cards are the *makadori* (matadors) and are followed by the Nines, Aces, the other three Jacks and Sixes of Clubs, Spades, Hearts and Diamonds, respectively. The 9♣ is commonly called *plägu* – literally, this means 'torture', because playing it may force the next player into leading a *makadori* he would rather have kept in reserve.

Unplayable cards are the remaining Eights, Tens, Queens and the other Kings, although the K♣ can score in a specific instance. Sevens have their own status. They are scoring cards and cannot be beaten, but they cannot beat other cards. They have no rank order.

THE DEAL

From the 36-card deck, each player receives nine cards (or six cards each if there are six people playing), dealt one at a time. Play is to the left.

PLAY

The player to the dealer's left leads, but first he lays any Sevens he may hold face up on the table. Each of these counts by itself as a trick. He then leads a playable card to the first trick. Each of the other players in turn must subsequently play a higher card if they can. If not, they must pass. The highest card played wins the trick and its winner leads to the next, assuming that he holds Sevens or playable cards. If not, the lead passes to the next player in clockwise rotation.

SCORING

Winning six tricks is worth a stroke. Winning six tricks in succession is known as a lurch (*jan*) and is worth two strokes. A no-score draw is a possible outcome.

CONCLUSION

Play continues until a partnership has won a score by taking six tricks – five if they hold the K♣. The latter feature is often called into play when playable cards have been exhausted and neither side has managed to take six tricks. If neither partnership succeeds in taking six tricks, there is no score and the same dealer deals again. Six strokes wins the game.

Below: The so-called playable cards in Brus, ranked in order from the highest to lowest.

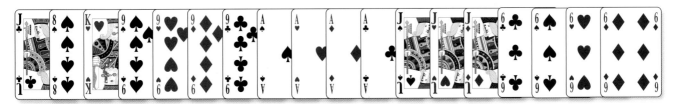

Left: The so-called unplayable cards in Brus. They are all unusable, except the K♣, which is the 'outcome card'. Possession of this decides some games which would otherwise be drawn.

ALKORT

This was Iceland's national card game until its place was usurped by Bridge. What adds spice to this game, which can trace its origins back to at least the 18th century, is its unusual card rankings and the fact that, before play starts, it is perfectly legal to show your partner your highest card.

OBJECT

To take as many tricks as possible. Five or more tricks need to be taken in order to win a game.

CARD RANKING

The cards rank as follows. The K♦ is highest, followed by a 2♥, 4♣, 8♠, 9♥ and 9♦, and then Aces, Jacks, Sixes and the remaining Eights, regardless of suit. The Queens, Threes, black Nines, and remaining Fours, Twos and Kings are valueless. The Sevens have a special status. When led to a trick, they are unbeatable, but otherwise they cannot beat another card. A Seven cannot be led unless its player has previously taken a trick.

THE DEAL

Players cut for partners and deal. From the 44-card deck, each receives nine cards three at a time; the remaining cards are placed face down to form the stock. If a player holds no card capable of beating an Eight, he may declare himself *friðufaer* (under eight). He shows all his cards, discards eight and takes eight from the stock.

PLAY

Before play, the partners secretly show each other the highest card in their hands. The player to the dealer's left leads to the first trick. The trick's winner leads to the next.

Left: This player holds no card capable of beating an Eight, so may declare himself *friðufaer* (under eight). To do this, he must show all his cards, and discard all but one of them, taking eight replacements from the stock.

You will need: Standard pack with Tens and Fives removed
Card ranking: See under 'Card Ranking' below
Players: Two, or four in partnerships of two, as described here
Ideal for: 14+

There is no need to follow suit, and the highest card played takes the trick. If two or more equally high cards are played, the one played first counts as highest.

SCORING

At least five out of the nine tricks need to be taken in order to score a game point. If a partnership takes five tricks before their opponents have taken one, they *múk* their opponents and score five points. If they win six or more tricks in this way, they make a stroke, scoring as many points as there are tricks in the stroke.

CONCLUSION

Play continues until all five tricks have been played for, unless one partnership has taken five tricks in succession. In this case, play continues for as long as it takes to win.

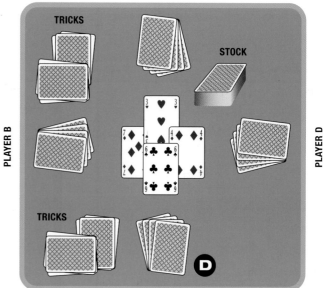

Above: Player B has led the 7♦. Sevens can only be led after having previously taken a trick, and, although worthless otherwise, when led they cannot be beaten, so Player B takes the trick.

11 | TAROT GAMES

CONTRARY TO POPULAR BELIEF, TAROT CARDS WERE NOT ORIGINALLY INVENTED FOR FORTUNE TELLING. THEY WERE INTRODUCED INTO THE ITALIAN CARD WORLD IN THE EARLY 15TH CENTURY AS A MEANS OF PEPPING UP TRICK-TAKING GAMES BY INTRODUCING A NEW INGREDIENT INTO THEM – THE NOTION OF TRUMPS. FROM THERE, TAROT GAMES SPREAD THROUGHOUT MUCH OF EUROPE, AND THEY ARE STILL POPULAR THERE TODAY.

The Italian idea was to add a fifth suit of 21 specially illustrated numbered cards called *trionfi* (triumphs) to the then standard pack of 56 cards bearing the standard Italian suitmarks of swords, staves, cups and coins, plus a special card called the Fool or *Excuse*. The original full pack therefore consisted of 78 cards. Despite appearances, the Fool is not the origin of the modern Joker. Originally, it was simply a card that could be played at any time, rather than following suit or trumping. It could not take a trick. Later, in Central Europe, its role changed and it became the highest trump.

The *trionfi* were trick-takers, and their original function was to act as cards that would beat any ordinary card played to the same trick. In English, *trionfi* was to become trumps, but Tarot games never really caught on in Britain in the same way as they did in Spain, Portugal and the Balkans, where they remain popular to this day. It was not until early in the 16th century that card players decided that it was simpler and more economical to pick a card at random from the existing pack and make its suit trumps, so doing away with the complexities of the separate *trionfi* suit. Slightly later, for reasons unknown, the Italians renamed *trionfi* as *tarocchi*. It is from this latter word, however, that the German word *tarock* is derived and subsequently the French and English word tarot.

Above: Most people associate Tarot cards with fortune telling, but, contrary to popular belief, they were not invented for that purpose.

FRENCH TAROT

This, as the name suggests, is the most popular Tarot game in France. The 78-card *Tarot Nouveau* deck consists of the four standard suits, a suit of 21 *atouts* (trumps) and the *Excuse* (the Fool). The *Excuse*, the One and Twenty-one of trumps, are known collectively as *bouts* (ends).

> **You will need:** 78-card *Tarot Nouveau* deck (see opposite)
>
> **Card ranking:** The 21 numbered trumps (from Twenty-one to One); the *Excuse* (depicting a Fool or Jester); the 14 cards in the four suits: King, Queen, Cavalier, Jack and Ten down to One
>
> **Players:** Four, in variable partnerships from hand to hand
>
> **Ideal for:** 14+

OBJECT

The soloist, the successful bidder, aims to win a minimum number of points, the amount of which depends on the number of *bouts* in the tricks he wins.

BIDDING AND THE SOLOIST

The person who will play alone as the soloist against the three others is decided by an auction. Starting with the player to the dealer's right, each player in turn has one opportunity to bid to win a certain number of points with their hand, or to pass. Each bid must be higher than the one preceding it. If all four players pass, the cards are thrown in and the next to deal deals a new hand.

The soloist's objective is to win a set number of points, which varies depending on the number of *bouts* that are contained in the tricks he takes. Three *bouts* means that the soloist needs at least 36 card points to win, two *bouts* requires 41 points to win, and one *bout* 51 points. With no *bouts*, at least 56 card points are needed to win. Each *bout* and King is worth five points, Queens four, Knights three and Jacks two.

DECLARATIONS

Before play, each player in turn can make one or more declarations. The points these score do not count towards winning a bid. They are scored in addition to what is won or lost. A player holding 10 or more trumps can declare *Poignée* (bunch). A single bunch scores 20 points (10–12 trumps), a double (13–14 trumps) 30 and a treble (15 trumps) 40. Declaring *Chelem* (slam) is an announcement of the intention to take all 18 tricks. If successful, it is worth 400 points; there is a 200-point penalty for failure. An undeclared *Chelem* scores 200 points and no penalties.

THE DEAL

Each player receives 18 cards in packets of three, with six cards being dealt face down to form the *chien* (dog). They can be dealt at any stage of the deal, but the first and last three cards of the pack cannot be included. A player who has been dealt the One of trumps and no other trump must declare the deal void. The cards are thrown in and the next dealer deals.

Right: Cards from the Marseilles Tarot pack, one of the standard patterns for the design of tarot cards accepted today. There are 21 trump cards, the first of which is the Magician (*le Bateleur*); the House of God, or Tower (*la Maison Dieu*), is the sixteenth trump. At times, the Fool (*le Mat*), is unnumbered and viewed as separate and additional to the other 21 numbered trumps.

LE BATELEUR
THE MAGICIAN

LA MAISON DIEU
THE TOWER OF DESTRUCTION

LE MAT
THE FOOL

Above: 17th-century French tarot cards: *La lune* (moon), *Le chariot* (chariot), *L'ermite* (hermit) and *Ivsttice* (justice), by an unknown Parisian manufacturer.

The four possible bids are as follows:

• *Petite* (small): if successful, its bidder can use the cards in the *chien* to improve his hand.

• *Garde* (guard): the same bid for a higher score. In both this and *Petite*, the soloist turns up and takes the cards in the *chien* and discards six cards from his hand face down. These discards may not include any trumps, Kings or the *Excuse*.

• *Garde Sans Chien* (guard without the dog): the taker plays without the benefit of the cards in the *chien*, although the card points in it still count towards his score

• *Garde Contre le Chien* (guard against the dog): the taker plays without the cards in the *chien,* and the card points in it go to the taker's opponents.

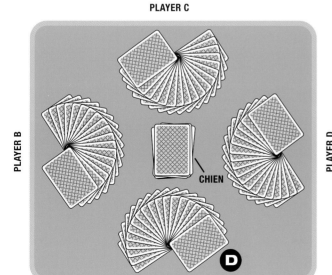

PLAY

The soloist takes the *chien* and discards, moving it to his side of the table if playing *sans le chien*, or, if the bid is *contre le chien*, moving it to the opposite player's side. The player to the dealer's right leads. Players must follow suit if they can, or trump or overtrump. If this is impossible, a trump must still be played even though it will not take the trick. The *Excuse* can be played at any time. It can also be retrieved from a taken trick and replaced by a worthless card. The *Excuse* cannot take a trick unless it is led to the last trick by a team that has won the 17 preceding ones.

SCORING AND CONCLUSION

At the end of the hand, the opponents pool their tricks. The last trick is worth 10 points (*Petit au Bout*) if it holds a One of trumps. The cards are counted in pairs of two non-scoring cards or a non-scoring card and a scoring one. The first scores a point, and the second is worth the scoring card's value. The total is deducted from 91 for the soloist's score. In a *Petite*, the score won or lost is 25 for game, plus the difference between the card points the soloist won and the number needed. The *Petit au Bout* is added or subtracted. In a *Garde*, the total is doubled; in *Garde Sans Chien* quadrupled and in *Garde Contre le Chien* sextupled. The *Poignée* and *Chelem* bonuses are added or subtracted. The soloist wins, or loses, this number of points from all three opponents.

Left: The remaining six cards in the pack, the *chien*, can be dealt at any stage of the deal, but must not include the first and last cards of the pack.

Ottocento

Originating in Bologna in the 16th century, hence its other name Tarocco Bolognese, this partnership game is still played there with a special 62-card pack also known as the *Tarocco Bolognese*. It consists of four 10-card suits (Swords, Batons, Coins and Cups), 21 trump cards, and a wild card called the *Matto*, which is not a trump and has no ranking order.

You will need: *Tarocco Bolognese* 62-card pack	
Card ranking: See box below	
Players: Four, in partnerships of two	
Ideal for: 14+	

Object

To be the first to score 800 points. There are four ways to score points: for card combinations in individual hands; for card combinations from tricks captured by each partnership; for individual counting cards captured in tricks by each partnership; and for winning the last trick.

The Deal

Who deals first is decided randomly, after which the deal passes to the right. The dealer shuffles the cards, and the player to his left cuts them. Each player receives 15 cards five at a time, the dealer discarding two from the seven he would otherwise be left with at the end of the deal. The discards count for the dealing partnership as though they were in tricks, but if the partnership loses every trick, they too are lost. The only cards that may not be discarded are the *Tarrochi* (see box) and the Kings.

Play

Immediately before playing to the first trick, each player in turn has the opportunity to declare any scoring combinations by placing the appropriate cards face up on the table. Otherwise, after this, the cards are picked up and returned to that player's hand. The alternative is to score them at the end of the hand. It is not compulsory to make declarations, nor need they be made in full. A player may declare a sequence of four cards, for instance, while actually holding five, without penalty. If either side scores 800 points through declarations alone, the game ends then, without any further play.

Any card may be led, the other players following suit or playing a trump, unless a player holds the *Matto*. This can be played regardless of whether its player holds any

---

Card Rankings Suit by Suit

Card rankings differ from suit to suit, as follows:

- In Swords and Batons, the highest-ranking card is the King, followed by Queen, Knight, Jack, Ten to Six and Ace.
- In Cups and Coins, it is King, Queen, Knight, Jack, Ace and then Six to Ten.
- Of the 21 trumps, *Angelo* (Angel) is the highest, followed by *Mondo* (World), *Sole* (Sun), *Luna* (Moon), Sixteen down to Five, the four *Mori cards* (Moors), and *Bègato*.

The cards from Sixteen down to Five also have names. They are:

- *Stella* (Star)
- *Saetta* (Thunderbolt)
- *Diavolo* (Devil)
- *Morte* (Death)
- *Traditore* (Traitor)
- *Vecchio* (Old Man)
- *Ruota* (Wheel)
- *Forza* (Strength)
- *Giustitia* (Justice)
- *Temperanza* (Temperament)
- *Carro* (Chariot)
- *Amore* (Love).

The *Matto* is not a trump and has no ranking order. *Angelo*, *Mondo*, *Bègato* and *Matto* are collectively termed *Tarrochi*.

Left: Aces from an Italian playing card set, of the Batons, Cups, Coins and Swords suits. Italian playing cards most commonly consist of a deck of 40 cards (four suits from One to Seven, plus three face cards). Since these cards first appeared in the late 17th century, when each region in Italy was a separately ruled province, there is no official Italian pattern.

cards of the suit led. It is always retained by the partnership playing it – if the opposing partnership takes the trick, it is simply exchanged for a worthless card. It can be lost only if the partnership playing it loses every trick.

Upon leading to a trick, a player can make three signals. *Vollo*, tossing a card in the air, means that this is the last card held in that particular suit. *Busso*, striking the table with the fist, is a signal to play the highest card held. *Striscio*, scraping a card on the table, is a request to lead trumps. It is acceptable to make more than one signal at the same time.

SCORING

The *Tarrochi* (*Angelo*, *Mondo*, *Bègato* and *Matto*) and Kings are worth five points, Queens four, Knights three, Jacks two and all other cards a point each. The winner of the last trick scores six extra points. The cards are counted in pairs, a point being deducted from each pair's value. Including the last trick, there are 93 points available in the pack.

To work out card points, a single one-point card is placed on top of each two-, three-, four-, or five-point one and the values scored. The remaining one-point cards are counted in pairs with the six-point bonus for taking the last trick being added, if appropriate. The other side's score is determined by subtracting the declaring partnership's total from the possible 93 points in the pack. The partnership to score 800 points first wins the rubber.

Below: Cards from the Visconti-Sforza deck, the earliest set of Tarot cards, which was produced in Italy in the mid-15th century. They were commissioned by Filippo Maria Visconti (1392–1447), Duke of Milan. The cards were then still called *trionfi* (trump) cards, From left to right, the cards are the Fool, the Hanged Man, the Magician, and the Empress.

Combinations of three or more cards of the same kind are called *cricche*. A *cricche* of all four *Tarocchi* is worth 36 points, while any three scores 18. Kings score 34 and 17 for four or three respectively, Queens 28 and 14, Knights 26 and 13 and Jacks 24 and 12. If three or more different *cricche* are scored at the same time, the total score is doubled. Combinations of three or more cards in sequence also score. A three-card sequence scores 10 points, with each additional card adding five points to that score.

This is where the *Matto* and *Bègato* shine. As wild cards, they can be used to establish a sequence or to extend one, but can only be used in trump sequences. They can then be used consecutively, except at the end of a sequence. If they are not needed to establish a sequence, they can be added to its length – and increase the score.

CONCLUSION

If any combinations are announced during the first trick, they are scored then. Otherwise, scoring takes place at the end of the hand. Usually, one partnership starts by laying out all the cards it has captured face up on the table, so as to show all the significant cards of each suit, trumps and *Mori* in rank order.

The *cricche* are counted first, remembering to double the score if there are more than three of them, followed by those of the opposing partnership. Sequences are then scored, and the scores are again doubled if there are three or more. Finally, the individual card points are calculated.

GLOSSARY

Aces High The term used when the Ace is the highest-ranked card in each suit. When it is the lowest-ranked, the term is **Aces Low**.

Alliance A temporary partnership between players that lasts for only one deal.

Ante In gambling games, the opening stake that all players must make before or at the start of each deal.

Auction Bidding to establish which suit should be trumps, how many tricks the bidders undertake to win and other basic conditions of a particular game.

Bid The offer to win a certain number of tricks in exchange for choosing conditions of play, for example, what the trump suit will be. If a bid is not overcalled by a higher one, then it becomes a contract.

Blank A term used in card-point games to describe a card that is valueless.

Boodle In the game Michigan, cards from a separate pack placed on a layout on which bets (gambling chips or counters) are staked.

Book In Bridge and Whist, the first six tricks won by a side, which are recorded 'below the line'. In collecting games, a set of four cards of the same rank.

Card-points The point-scoring values of specific cards, principally in point-trick games. These points are different to the nominal face values.

Carte blanche A hand containing no court cards.

Carte rouge A hand in which every card counts towards a scoring combination.

Chip Counter which is used to represent money. Also called a gambling chip.

Combination A set of scoring cards that match each other in rank or by suit.

Court cards The King, Queen and Jack of each suit, as opposed to the numbered or 'pip' cards. They are also sometimes referred to as picture cards.

Cut To divide a pack of playing cards by lifting a portion from the top, to establish who deals first.

Deadwood Penalty cards remaining in opponents' hands when a player goes out.

Deal The distribution of cards to the players at the beginning of a game and the play ensuing between one deal and the next.

Declare To state the contract or conditions of play (for example, the trump suit or number of tricks intended, etc.). To reveal your hand and score for achieving a particular combination of cards.

Declarer The highest bidder in an auction, who then tries to fulfil his contract.

Deuce The Two of any suit.

Discard A card that a player has rejected and placed on a discard pile. To throw away a worthless or unwanted card to a trick.

Draw To take or be dealt one or more cards from a stock or discard pile.

Dummy A full hand of cards dealt to the table, or, in Bridge, to one of the players (who has to spread them face up on the table at a certain point in the game), with which the declarer plays as well as with his own hand.

Elder/Eldest The player who is obliged to lead, bid or make the opening bet first, usually the person seated to the left of the dealer in left-handed games, or seated to the right in right-handed games.

Exchange To discard cards and receive the same number of replacements or to add cards to a hand and then discard the same number.

Flush A hand of cards that are all of the same suit.

Follow suit To play a card of the same suit as the last one played.

Game The whole series of deals, or the target score. For example, 'game is 500 points'.

Game points Card points that are won to fulfill a particular bid.

Go out To play the last card of a hand.

Hand The cards held by each player or the play that takes place between one deal and the next.

Head To play a higher card than any so far played to the trick.

Hole cards The cards dealt face down to each player which remain unseen by the other players, until the end of the game.

Honours Cards that attract bonus scores or extra payments if they are held in hand and, occasionally, if captured in play.

Joker An extra card supplied with the standard 52-card pack that is often used as a wild card.

Kitty Another term for the pool or pot of chips that are being played for.

Knock In Rummy, a player uses this to signify that all his cards are melded. In Poker, knocking can be used to signify that a player will make no more bets.

Laying off The playing of cards to opponents' melds on the table in Rummy games.

Lead The first card to be played or the action of playing the first card.

Maker The player who names the trump suit.

Marriage A meld of the King and Queen of the same suit.

Meld A group of cards of the same rank or in sequence that attracts scores or privileges.

Misdeal To deal cards incorrectly, in which case they must be collected, shuffled and dealt again.

Misère A contract to lose every trick in a hand, otherwise termed a *Null*.

Null A contract to lose every trick in a hand, or a card carrying no point value in point-trick games.

Ouverte A contract played with one's hand of cards spread face up on the table for everyone to see.

Overcall To bid higher than the previous bidder.

Overtrick A trick taken in excess of the number a player is contracted to take.

Pair Two cards of the same rank.

Pass To miss a turn when it comes to bidding or playing without dropping out of play.

Plain suit A suit other than the trump suit.

Pool/Pot This is a sum of money or an agreed equivalent, such as a number of chips, to which the players contribute before play starts or throughout play and which is taken by the eventual winner.

Prial Three cards of the same rank; a triplet.

Quint In Piquet, a set of five cards. In Quinto, the Five of every suit, and every pair of cards in a suit that totals five. In this game, the Joker is known as the Quint Royal.

Raise In Poker, to increase the level of a bet, usually by calling the previous bet and then wagering at least the same amount again.

Rank A card's denomination and its relative trick-taking power (for example, 'Ace ranks above King').

Renege To fail to follow suit to the card led, but legally, in accordance with the rules of the game.

Revoke To fail to follow suit, when able and required to do so. It usually incurs a penalty if detected.

Round A division of play in which every player participates in dealing, bidding, playing a trick, etc. the same number of times (usually once).

Rubber In partnership games, a match usually consisting of three games and thus won by the side winning two.

Ruff In games of Bridge, playing a trump card on a trick that was led with a plain suit. In Gleek, it is the highest card value a player holds in a single suit

Run Another term for a sequence.

Sequence A run of three or more cards of the same suit in rank or numerical order.

Shoe A box from which cards are dealt in some card games.

Slam A bid to win every trick in a hand.

Solo A contract played with the hand as dealt without exchanging any cards, or, played alone against the other players. The soloist is the player who elects to play alone.

Stake The amount of money or chips a player is willing to play with during a game, or the amount a player needs to be included in a game.

Stock The cards that are not dealt immediately to the players, but may be dealt or drawn from later on during the game.

Suit The internationally recognized suits are Hearts, Clubs, Diamonds and Spades. There are also local ones found in German, Italian and Spanish games.

Talon The undealt portion of the pack put aside for use later in a game; the same as the stock.

Three of a Kind Three cards of the same rank.

Trey The Three of any suit.

Trick A round of cards, consisting of one from each player in turn, played according to the rules of the particular game.

Trump A suit that outranks all the others. A trump card always beats any card from a plain suit.

Turn-up A card, also called the upcard, turned up at the start of play to determine which suit is trumps and, depending on the game, at other times during play for a variety of reasons.

Undertrick A trick which is less than the number bid or contracted.

Upcard Another term for the turn-up card.

Void Having no cards of a specified suit.

Vole The winning of every trick; same as slam.

Vulnerable In Bridge, this describes a partnership, which, having won one game towards the rubber, is subject to increased scores or penalties.

Waste pile A pile of unwanted cards, usually dealt face up.

Widow A hand of cards dealt to the table face down usually at the start of play which players may exchange cards with during the game.

Wild card A card that can stand in for any other card, either played freely or subject to certain restrictions, depending on the game.

Younger/Youngest The player last in turn to bid or play at the beginning of a game.

INDEX

PICTURE CREDITS

We would like to thank the following for kindly supplying photographs for this book. Images are listed in clockwise order (t = top, c = centre, b = bottom, l = left, r = right). **akg-images** 69tr. **Alamy** 7br, 24br, 42br, 50br, 62br, 74br, 96bl, 110br, 113tr, 113cl, 121br. **BBco** 2, 12br, 80br, 96tr, 122b, 125b. **Bridgeman Art Library** 59tr, 124br. **Corbis** 8br, 9tr, 19cl, 29br, 36bl, 77bl, 114tr. **Dover Publications Inc.** 8tl, 24tl, 39b, 41tr, 42tl, 50tl, 51br, 62tl, 70tl, 74tl, 82tl, 94tl, 116tl, 123t. **Getty Images** 6tr, 82br, 103bl. **iStock** 95bl. **The Kobal Collection** 94br. **Mary Evans Picture Library** 6bl, 7tl, 13, 70br, 116br. **Photos.com** 31tr. **Topfoto** 61bl.